ROCK, RHYTHM & BLUES

For Ding,
Enjoy Rock n roll
history ... "Philly"
style!

Jim Rosin

A Look at the National Recording Artists from the City of Brotherly Love

James Rosin

Published by the Autumn Road Company
Philadelphia, Pennsylvania

Library of Congress Control Number 2004103903

ISBN 0-9728684-1-0

Book Design by Elizabeth S. Emery and Phyllis Pilla
Graphics by TinaMarie Owens

Printed by George H Buchanan, Bridgeport, NJ

Front Cover Photo: **Charlie Gracie**
Back Cover Photo: **Frankie Avalon**

TABLE OF CONTENTS

AUTHOR'S NOTE

This book was compiled from historical facts, statistics and information in the public domain. It was supplemented by interviews with recording artists and those closely associated with the music industry during the time covered.

This book is dedicated to **Dick Clark and American Bandstand** who (said Ray Smith), in an age of conformity, gave teens music to dance to, friends to hang out with, and a party in their living room.

ACKNOWLEDGMENTS

I would like to express my appreciation to all of the people who took time to help me put this book together: Dave Appell, Ed Hurst, Dick Richards, Charlie Gracie, James Darren, Fabian, Bobby Rydell, Arlene Sullivan, Bob Marcucci, Kenny Rossi, Ray Smith, Peter Ford, Lew Klein, Marvin Brooks, Jerry Gross, Mark Stevens, Joe Niagara, Jerry Blavat, Stephen Caldwell, Al "Caesar" Berry, Joe Fusco, Nino Bambino, Barbara Marcen, Mary Ann Colella and Bobbi Young.

Also thanks to Dick Clark, Fred Bronson and their book, Dick Clark's American Bandstand; Norm N. Nite and his book, Rock On: The Illustrated Encyclopedia of Rock 'n' Roll; Richard Rosin; Holly Drauglis and the Philadelphia Music Alliance; Jason Ankeny, Andrew Hamilton, Bruce Eder, Steve Huey, Ed Hogan and all music.com; Randye Jones and Afrocentric Voices in Classical Music; LaRissa Douglas, Ben Scantlin, Lauren Ito and Chancellor Entertainment; Broadcast Pioneers; History Makers; history-of-rock.com; geatorgold.net; Temple University's Urban Archives; Aliya Crawford and W&W Public Relations; Mars Talent Agency; the Richard De Le Font Agency and Val Shively and Chuck Dabagian of R&B Records. (They have the largest selection of 45 rpms in the country.) Visit them at 49 Garrett Road in Upper Darby, PA or call 610-352-2320.

Foreword

Growing up in Philadelphia in the late 1950s and early 1960s was much different than today. Teenagers of that era didn't have all of the choices and alternatives that the young people have now. What they did have were parents who offered guidance, neighborhood grownups who looked out for them, the playground where they played ball, the Saturday matinee, the bowling alleys, and parties in the basement where they danced to rock 'n' roll.

The music was new and brought an excitement and abandon that allowed teens to step outside the rules and regulations of that time. The transistor radio, portable record player and 45 rpm gave them freedom to do that. It also gave them a voice that the adult world began to listen to. Dick Clark and American Bandstand were there to ensure they heard the music of Bill Haley and His Comets, Elvis, Little Richard, Chuck Berry, Jerry Lee Lewis, Buddy Holly, The Everly Brothers and Fats Domino.

Today when many listen to the oldies with the rich vocal harmony and fundamental back beat, they go back to a simpler, gentler, more innocent time. In the somewhat cold and corporate world of today, that's something nice for people to remember.

**In Memory of
Joe Niagara**

"Up there, where the air is rare,
the Rockin' Bird will fly. . . ."

"People always tell you
to live in the present.
Be in the moment.
Don't live in the past.
But I don't mind goin'
back there. A lot of good
things happened to me
then . . . ."

Stephen Caldwell
(The Orlons)

THE FATHER OF ROCK 'N' ROLL

In the early 1950s, a new form of music began to emerge. It evolved from the black rhythm and blues bands that featured artists such as Joe Turner, Jimmy Rushing, and Wynonie Harris, who took the big-band sound of the 1940s and added rhythm to it.

The new music was driven by guitars, drums, and had a distinct sound. There was a mixed reaction, but most agreed that it wasn't destined to last very long.

Rock 'n' Roll music faced plenty of adversity when first introduced. Many thought it was obscene and vulgar. Religious leaders spoke out against it. Even people in the recording industry condemned it. Yet there were people who were inspired by the passion and freedom inherent in the music.

The first rock 'n' roll record was probably "Rocket 88" recorded by Jackie Brenston and His Delta Cats, or "Boogie Woogie Blues" recorded by Charlie Gracie in 1951. The first rock 'n' roll group to record a series of hits and tap into the musical mainstream was Bill Haley and His Comets.

Bill Haley, known as the "father of rock 'n' roll," played rock music long before it became fashionable. Originally from Highland Park, Michigan, Haley moved to Chester (outside of Philadelphia) as a child. His parents were both musicians who encouraged him to sing and play guitar.

By the late 1940s, Haley had formed a group called the Saddlemen with John Grande (accordion), Al Rex (bass), and Billy Williamson (steel guitar).

In 1951, the group recorded the rhythm and blues tune "Rocket 88" that was originally recorded by Jackie Brenston. Haley boosted the rhythm section, and added some lead guitar. Their recording was regarded by many as the first "white band rock 'n' roll song." Haley began to attract a young audience that liked his R&B style of music. His next release (on Dave Miller's Essex Records) was "Rock the Joint," a tune with a catchy phrase and a notable guitar solo by Danny Cedrone. The record sold well in Cleveland and it caught the attention of DJ Alan Freed.

DICK RICHARDS
(DRUMMER, BILLY HALEY AND
HIS COMETS 1953-55)

The group was doing a radio show with Alan Freed in Cleveland in early 1952, and Freed played this record: "Rock the Joint." He became so inspired by the phrases "Rock, Rock, Rock Everybody," "Roll, Roll, Roll Everybody," that at one point he said to his audience, "Let's rock 'n' roll to Bill Haley's 'Rock the Joint.'" He must have played it a dozen times and began to get requests to play the "rock 'n' roll tune." That was how the term got popularized.

By 1953 the group now known as Bill Haley and His Comets had their first major hit with "Crazy Man Crazy," again on Essex. In 1954, the group changed labels and went to Decca Records.

RICHARDS

Our first record there that April was a song called "Thirteen Women (and Only One Man in Town)." That was tagged as the "A" side. The flip side was a tune called "(We're Gonna) Rock Around the Clock." The irony was in a 3-hour recording session, we spent 2 ½ hours on "Thirteen Women" and did "Rock Around the Clock" in two takes. When the record came out, they pushed "Thirteen Women," and both songs didn't do much. So Decca got us back into a recording session right away. There was an R&B tune out by Joe Turner called "Shake, Rattle and Roll." No one played it because the lyrics were sexual and suggestive. So Bill changed the lyric, the arrangement, and Joey Ambrose's saxophone gave it a new sound. The song made the top ten, sold a million copies, and put us on the map. I believe that was the first time a rock 'n' roll song was that successful. Later that year, we did it again with "Dim Dim the Lights."

In early 1955 the group recorded "Mambo Rock," "Birth of the Boogie," and were on tour in New England. Decca brought them home to record "Razzle Dazzle" and "Two Hound Dogs," to take advantage of their momentum. Then an unforeseen thing happened.

RICHARDS

Movie director Richard Brooks (a native Philadelphian) was finishing a picture at MGM called "Blackboard Jungle" with Glenn Ford, Sidney Poitier, Vic Morrow and Ann Francis. The film was about troubled and rebellious youth in a high school. Juvenile delinquency was a hot topic and this movie promised to create some attention. It happened that Glenn Ford's son Peter was a big

RICHARDS (Cont'd)

music fan and had some of our recordings. And this created a unique set of circumstances.

PETER FORD

In the fall of 1954, I was a precocious fifth grader who loved rhythm and blues. Between the Beverly Hills Music Shop and Wallach's Music City at Sunset and Vine, I was a busy lad indulging myself. One of the records I bought was "Thirteen Women (and Only One Man in Town)." Earlier, I had purchased "Crazy Man Crazy," and knew that this Haley fellow was on to something. When I brought "Thirteen Women" home and played it, I didn't like it. I turned the record over to discover the real A-side: "(We're Gonna) Rock Around the Clock." How Decca Records could have thought that "Thirteen Women" could have been the A-side was a mystery to me. When my father was signed to star in "Blackboard Jungle," Richard Brooks (the director-screenwriter) would stop by our house to visit Dad and talk about the production. It was on one of these visits that he heard some of my records and borrowed them, one of which was "Rock Around the Clock" (RATC). Toward the end of production, Brooks and his assistant director, Joel Freeman, listened to three songs and agreed that Haley's up-tempo "Jump Blues" tune was the perfect choice. MGM purchased the rights to "RATC" for $5,000 from Decca Records with the condition that they could only use the music three times in the film. Brooks would now use the music in the beginning of the film over the opening credits, as well as at the end. Since MGM had paid for another opportunity, the studio cleverly used strains and riffs from "RATC" intermixed with jazz music during a fight scene. In February of 1955, a

FORD (Cont'd)

sneak preview was scheduled at the Encino Theater
in the San Fernando Valley. As an early tenth
birthday surprise, my father asked me if I'd like to
go. We snuck into the theater just as it was about to
begin. I remember very clearly my thoughts as the
first scene opened on the empty blackboard as the
credits rolled by: Wow! Not only were they playing
"Rock Around the Clock," the song that Dad had
borrowed from my record collection and given to
Mr. Brooks, but it was so loud — just like I played
it at home. It was wonderful! There couldn't have
been a happier kid in the whole world than me at
that moment!

RICHARDS

All of a sudden, the record had a new identity. Kids
were dancin' in the aisles of movie theaters. "Rock
Around the Clock" shot up to No. 1 in the world.
Our latest recording "Razzle Dazzle," which was
supposed to be a huge hit, was completely over-
shadowed by a song we recorded a year before that
we considered dead as a doornail. And that song
became the largest selling single record in rock 'n'
roll history. I think it's sold about 200 million
copies.

An interesting problem the group faced when they began to
get popular was their concerts never sounded like their recording
sessions.

RICHARDS

In concert we had Joey Ambrose on sax, Billy
Williamson on steel guitar, Johnny Grande on
accordion, Marshall Lytle on bass, Bill on lead
guitar, and myself on drums. But Bill was never
really a lead guitarist. We had a lot of life and

RICHARDS (Cont'd)

"zippitty doo-dah," but it never sounded like the band that recorded. I think it was because Danny Cedrone, our studio guitarist never played with us in concert. He had his own band. But then Danny had an accidental death in 1954, right after the terrific guitar work he did on "Rock Around the Clock." So Bill hired Franny Beecher who had played with the Benny Goodman orchestra, to do our recording sessions. When Franny became our lead guitarist, that gave us the voicing (harmony) between sax and guitar, and in turn, gave us that basic sound that complemented the rhythm and vitality we already had. At that point, our concert and recording sounds were the same.

In late 1955, after a string of hit records, Joey Ambrose, Dick Richards, and Marshall Lytle left the group. They formed Jodimars (taken from their first names) and signed with Capitol Records. Their first recording was the hit "Now Dig This." Eventually they became one of the top lounge acts in Las Vegas and Reno.

Bill Haley had one more mega hit with "See You Later Alligator" in 1956. But by the late 1950s, Haley was no longer recording hit songs. He was able to remain active through the 1960s. Then in 1974, a rock 'n' roll revival boosted his popularity once again. "(We're Gonna) Rock Around the Clock," heard on the TV show "Happy Days" hit the charts again and placed in the top 40. Haley continued touring through the 1970s and passed away in 1981.

It was Bill Haley and His Comets who introduced a new style of music and opened the door for many rock 'n' roll groups to follow.

In the late 1980s the original Comets who recorded all of the group's major hits in the mid-1950s, reunited. Johnny Grande, Joey Ambrose, Dick Richards, Marshall Lytle, and Franny Beecher have performed to sold-out audiences all over the United States and Europe for the past 15 years. The original Comets are still "rockin' around the clock."

THE 950 CLUB

In early 1952, the WFIL TV station, located at 46th and Market in West Philadelphia, looked to make a program change. Their afternoon movies were a ratings bust and a replacement was needed.

WFIL had been airing a weekly music show called the TV Teen Club. It was hosted by Paul Whiteman, the well-known, heavy-set band leader. Every Saturday night, Whiteman invited local teens to dance on his show.

Management got the idea to produce an afternoon music show that would simulcast (air on radio and TV simultaneously) Monday through Friday. TV Teen Club was not their original source of inspiration. There was a program on WPEN (950) — the top pop radio station in the city of Philadelphia, called the 950 Club. The show was hosted by Joe Grady and Ed Hurst and originated back in the mid-1940s. The 950 Club was the first radio show where an invited studio teenage audience danced to the records played on the air.

ED HURST
(HOST OF 950 CLUB)
Our first show was at 1528 Walnut Street which was an office building. We broadcast from the 22nd Floor in a studio built on springs. But the kids would stuff the mailboxes, jam the elevators and run wild. So we were asked to leave. We relocated to a two-story building at 2212 Walnut Street.

HURST (Cont'd)

There we had a studio on the second floor, with an
auditorium, studio and luncheonette on the first
floor. We played the top pop tunes, and had
celebrity guests. There were talk shows in the
morning and we did the 950 Club in the afternoon.

The 950 Club quickly became Philadelphia's number-one
radio show and averaged two to three thousand pieces of fan mail
each week.

Meanwhile, WFIL took notice of Grady and Hurst. Their
show had earned a Hooper-Pulse rating with a 13 share, which was
unheard of against the soap opera competition. So they decided to
recruit the dynamic duo.

HURST

We walked into Roger Clipp's office (V.P. and
G.M. of WFIL) and were told we would start the
show in two weeks. Clipp asked for our salary
demands and adjourned the meeting. On the cab
ride back to WPEN I was floating on a cloud. But
Joe had this long face. I said, "What's with you?
We just got an offer you get once in a lifetime. A
chance to do a show on both radio and TV. We
can't miss." To which Joe replied, "You think
WPEN is going to let us out of our contract?"
Being young, naive and hopeful, I couldn't imagine
them standing in our way. So I went to the station
manager at WPEN and explained to him the
wonderful opportunity that awaited us. Without
blinking an eye, he said, "Okay, we'll let you
know." The next day we got a call from the
program manager at WFIL. I'll never forget his
choice of words. "We find this is not a propitious
time to bring you boys here." What happened was

HURST (Cont'd)

Bill Sylk, the owner of Sun Ray Drugs (the parent company of WPEN) called Walter Annenberg who owned WFIL and the Philadelphia Inquirer, and said, "If you attempt to raid our talent pool, I will personally withdraw one million dollars in endorsements from the Inquirer, and give it to the Philadelphia Bulletin." That was the end of that.

BANDSTAND

Unable to sign Grady and Hurst, WFIL set their sights on someone in their own backyard: Bob Horn. Horn was a 37-year-old radio personality from nearby Reading. He had hosted a very popular program at night on WIP and later on WPEN, called Bandstand, where he played the current pop tunes.

Now on WFIL radio, Horn was anxious to make the move to afternoon TV. Roger Clipp was also anxious to make use of a collection of musical film shorts gathering dust on the shelf. So in September of 1952, Bob Horn hosted an afternoon TV show at 3 P.M. weekdays called "Parade of Stars" that combined the dated musical film shorts with his commentary, and an occasional guest.

LEW KLEIN
(EXECUTIVE PRODUCER OF
AMERICAN BANDSTAND, 1957-63)
I was a staff director then and I did some of Bob Horn's afternoon shows. We did them in Studio C, a converted radio studio with one camera. Bob would sit at a desk, introduce the film shorts that featured artists like Nat King Cole, Peggy Lee and George Shearing, and then do commentary. At the same time, kids from the two nearby high schools who knew Bob from listening to his radio show, began to come by the studio to visit and talk with him. They would dance to the musical shorts, but were never shown on camera. As more kids came by, someone turned the camera on them and punched it up on the air. Eventually the shorts got less air time and the teens got more.

As more kids began to approach the studio, Horn lobbied to revise the show and make it more like the format done by Grady and Hurst. The show was moved to the larger Studio B. To capitalize on Horn's successful radio show, WFIL named the new program "Bandstand."

The show premiered on October 6, 1952 and aired Monday through Friday from 3:30 to 4:45 P.M. Bandstand was produced on a very modest budget. The set was basic. Horn stood behind a wedge-shaped, elevated podium with a counter top.   Behind the counter was a painted backdrop that resembled the interior of a record shop. To the left were high school banners and standard wooden bleachers. To the right were additional banners hung on a bulletin board, and an open area used for guest performers. In the middle was an open dance floor. The studio held about 200 teens.

MARVIN BROOKS
(BANDSTAND CAMERAMAN, 1953-63)
We used three black and white RCA cameras. The center camera was on a dolly that would raise and lower it. We used this camera for the podium 'cause it would raise up high enough to shoot over the heads of the kids dancing and directly on the podium which sat on a platform. It could also be lowered and used to shoot guest artists who appeared to the right. The other two cameras were used for dancers and talent.

Bob Horn was given a co-host (to emulate Grady and Hurst) named Lee Stewart. Stewart was a pleasant little man with a crewcut and dark-rimmed glasses. The management thought

Stewart would provide comic relief but that never materialized. In fact, the two were a mismatch from the start. But having a co-host provided some advantages. If Horn had to prepare for a commercial or leave the set for some reason, there was coverage. Stewart remained on the show for a while and was eventually let go.

Bandstand drew its teenage audience initially from two nearby high schools on Chestnut Street: West Catholic High School for Girls and West Catholic High School for Boys. As time progressed, teens came from Bartram, West Philadelphia, South Philadelphia, Northeast and Lincoln high schools. No one was sure how the audience would react to the new dance show, but Bandstand was successful from the start.

Once inside the studio kids observed a strict dress code enforced by producer Tony Mammarella. It was sport coats or sweaters and ties for the boys, and skirts or dresses for the girls. No open shirts or tight sweaters were allowed.

KLEIN

A lot of the girls would come from Catholic school in their uniforms. Well, the nuns frowned on the girls dancing in their uniforms on Bandstand. So the kids would put on sweaters to cover the tops of their uniforms and the little collars stuck out. This was called the Peter Pan collar and became a fashion trend all over Philadelphia. When the show went network, poodle skirts, socks, shoes, a particular hairstyle — anything that the regulars wore — became a standard around the country for kids watching.

KENNY ROSSI
(AMERICAN BANDSTAND
REGULAR 1957-1958)

When I was on the show, my father, who was a
tailor, bought me a pair of these shoes that looked
like off-color white bucks. I thought they were
ugly, but they were the only pair of shoes I had, so I
wore them. Within a week, everyone wanted to
know where I got them and these shoes became a
fashion fad.

Bandstand looked for attractive kids who were good
dancers and well-behaved. An inner core of the best dancers who
came every day and received the most amount of fan mail became
part of "The Committee." The leader of the committee was a 14-
year-old (actually 13 years old then), named Jerry Blavat.

JERRY BLAVAT
(BANDSTAND REGULAR 1953-56)

I was asked to be there every day. It became my
job to rotate kids on the dance floor, and make sure
everyone who was a guest on the show got their
time on the floor. We also helped make sure that
everyone was respectful and observed the rules.
We danced to pop tunes like "No, Not Much" (Four
Lads), "Teach Me Tonight" (DiCastro Sisters),
"Unchained Melody" (Al Hibbler), and "Sincerely"
(McGuire Sisters). Bob would have guest artists
like Frankie Laine, Joni James, and Georgia Gibbs,
who would lip-sync their latest release.

The two most popular dances became the "Jitterbug" and
the "Slow Dance". The "Jitterbug" evolved from the "Lindy", a
spirited swing dance of the 1940s. A number of dance crazes

would develop on Bandstand. One of the earliest was the "Bunny Hop" that originated from the instrumental by Ray Anthony. The "Bunny Hop" was a bouncy dance that became a national hit. Dancers would line up, place their hands on the hips of the person in front of them, heel-toe left and right twice, jump forward, backward, then forward three times, and repeat the process.

ARLENE SULLIVAN
(AMERICAN BANDSTAND
REGULAR - 1957-60)

We were always looking to do new dances and try something different. Some of them were created or brought to us by kids on the show. Frankie Lobis introduced us to "The Stroll." A line of boys and girls would face each other. Then each couple at the head of the line would stroll down the aisle doing their little dance step. Each couple would try to outdo the other, and show off a bit. We had a lot of fun with that dance.

JOE FUSCO
(AMERICAN BANDSTAND
REGULAR - 1957-59)

Frankie Lobis and I used to go to the candy stores in the black community where they had juke boxes, and watch kids dance. We marveled at the way they moved and they taught us. One dance I brought back to the show was "The Strand." You could do it to a slow dance or half-time fast dance. You would push your partner out to the left or right in a backstep, then pull her back to a slow dance position, and keep moving as you did it.
Sometimes you would spin your partner in a circle, dance around her, then fall back into the dance.

FUSCO (Cont'd)
There was a little more detail and variation to it but that was basically it.

SULLIVAN
After the twist became popular in the early 1960s, dancing really began to change. A lot of new dances caught on where you danced apart and never touched. When you did the "Pony," "Swim," Watusi," or "Fish" you had a partner but it was really a solo dance.

Horn and Stewart also initiated dance contests and a weekly segment called "Record Review." (Later called Rate-A-Record on American Bandstand.) Three teens were picked to listen to a new song and asked to give it a numerical rating. (Between 35 and 98 in the Dick Clark era.) They judged it according to how good the beat was and how easy it was to dance to. The kids were usually right about what would be a hit.

BLAVAT
The preference of the Bandstand audience was pop music which held true through the mid-1950s. But in 1954, Bill Haley and His Comets had two mega hits with "Shake, Rattle and Roll" and "Dim, Dim the Lights." Bob Horn was very music-savvy and knew rock 'n' roll was gaining momentum. So he began to play R&B music with increasing regularity.

By 1955, Bob Horn had developed and hosted a local hit TV show. He was one of the most popular broadcast personalities in the city of Philadelphia. But in 1956 all that Horn had accomplished began to unravel. A drunk-driving arrest led to his suspension from the show, and later allegations of sexual misconduct led to his departure. (He was later acquitted.)

Tony Mammarella, the producer, filled in as host. Mammarella, a South Philadelphian and graduate of St. Joe's, came to WFIL in 1950. He was personable, responsible, intelligent, and knew most of the kids. But management preferred him to produce, and looked elsewhere for a replacement. The man most favored was Dick Clark, the 26-year-old host of "Caravan of Music," an afternoon show on WFIL Radio. Originally from Mt. Vernon, New York, Clark graduated from Syracuse University with a degree in communications. After working at WOLF Radio in Syracuse, Clark was hired by WKTV in Utica where he became a TV host. His desire to work in a larger city led him to WFIL in Philadelphia. Eventually, Clark was given his own afternoon radio show which aired from 2 PM to 6 PM weekdays.

Clark also became an experienced TV commercial announcer in his early days at WFIL. He pitched Tootsie Rolls (for Paul Whiteman's TV Teen Club) and spoke for Barr's Diamond Jewelers, WhiteCross Mattresses, and later a host of other products such as hair tonic, chewing gum and soda. In fact, he later helped line up enough sponsors to make American Bandstand one of daytime TV's most profitable shows.

BROOKS

An interesting thing about Dick was his recall ability. When he became host, we would do 8 to 10 different commercials, and we had no teleprompters or cue cards. So he used a Webcor tape recorder hidden under the commercial set. With an earpiece, he'd record his own voice doing the commercial, then play it back with a foot pedal. His voice would play in his ear and he'd repeat what he heard so he wouldn't miss a line. Very difficult to do. Most people couldn't speak and listen to themselves. But Dick did and never made a mistake. And those commercials were live and done quickly.

In July of 1956, Dick Clark became the host of Bandstand.

DICK CLARK

I had barely gotten over the shock of the sudden promotion from radio disc jockey to television host, when the studio was besieged by an angry crowd of teens with picket signs. They were mad because I was replacing Bob Horn. We were minutes away from going on the air when I walked outside to confront about two dozen picketers, furiously waving their signs. I introduced myself. No response. I acknowledged their feelings about Bob, but told them there was nothing I could do about it, and hoped they didn't dislike me because I was chosen to replace him. More silence. I invited them in and went back inside. No one followed. With two minutes to go, producer Tony Mammarella gave me the good news. The kids had dropped their picket signs and came into the studio. I had survived my first crisis as the host of Bandstand.[1]

[1]From Dick Clark's American Bandstand, HarperCollins, 1997.

BROOKS

Dick was a perfect fit as host. He was nice-looking, clean-cut, youthful, and had a great rapport with the kids on the show. He even looked like one of them. He worked hard to learn about the new kind of music he played and the artists who recorded it.

CLARK

I wasn't that knowledgeable about rock and roll when I first became the host of Bandstand, because I hadn't been allowed to play rock on my radio show. I had to stick to adult pop music playing artists like Perry Como and Rosemary Clooney. But hosting Bandstand was like taking a crash course in a new culture. I learned quickly — not just the facts about the music — but genuinely to love the music. As I became more familiar with the artists and the music, Tony Mammarella and I would alternate. One day he would pick the music and the next day I would make the selections.[1]

RAY SMITH
(CONTRIBUTING WRITER: DICK CLARK'S AMERICAN BANDSTAND)

As the show progressed, Dick Clark displayed a unique talent of taking the music that America was afraid of — rock and roll — and broadcasting it for teens who loved it, while introducing it to the adults who didn't.[1]

FRED BRONSON
(AUTHOR: THE BILLBOARD BOOK OF NUMBER ONE HITS)

1956 was a watershed year in the music industry. While artists like Bill Haley and Elvis Presley

[1]From <u>Dick Clark's American Bandstand</u>, HarperCollins, 1997.

BRONSON (Cont'd)

reached the top of the charts, much of the music on radio was still pop, not rock. But by year's end, you had more hits by artists like Fats Domino and Ivory Joe Hunter, alongside pop singers like Frank Sinatra and Patti Paige. It was a time of transition, and Bandstand contributed by playing all of the hits on the chart.[1]

KLEIN

In 1957, we began to feel we could be a bigger show and reach a wider audience. At the same time, ABC was looking to replace an afternoon movie with a new program. They agreed to give us a trial run, but they wanted a number of changes. The basic ones we agreed to were: we changed the name to American Bandstand; we changed the set, replacing the canvas backdrop of the record shop with gold records, and album covers on a dark green wooden background with dividers; and we altered the lighting.

[1]From <u>Dick Clark's American Bandstand</u>, HarperCollins, 1997.

AMERICAN BANDSTAND

American Bandstand debuted on the ABC network on
August 5, 1957. The show aired locally from 2:30 to 3 P.M.,
nationally from 3 P.M. to 4:30 P.M., and locally again from 4:30
P.M. to 5:00 P.M. The show was now shown on 48 stations
across the country and seen by millions of viewers. But a problem
arose right away. From 1952 to 1956 Bandstand was all-white. In
1957 Clark and Mammarella brought in black teenagers who
wanted to dance on the show.

KLEIN
When we began our network run, some of the
southern stations refused to carry us because we
were racially mixed. We didn't want to change that
but this was a risk. Not every affiliate carried us.
And we needed every station we could get to stay
on the network. So we had a meeting and made a
decision we thought was the right thing to do. We
told those southern stations: "If you don't like the
makeup of our show, don't carry us."

Within a month, American Bandstand was such a hit that
the majority of affiliates carried the show and more were signing
up. People all over the country were talking about Dick Clark and
American Bandstand.

SMITH
When Bandstand went national, it was the first time
the teenagers across the country heard the same
music at the same time. In effect, that legitimized

SMITH (Cont'd)

the music and secured the teenage place in society. Now teenagers had their own music, separate from their parents. In a sense, Dick was a visionary: he had the innate ability to sense change and capitalized on it.

FRANK MAFFEI
(DANNY AND THE JUNIORS)

It was definitely Dick Clark who helped make it come true. By sensing Bandstand was much more than a local show and pushing for network airing, he brought rock 'n' roll into households nationwide and made it part of the pop culture.

BRONSON

An important reason why American Bandstand impacted the country was the music was made presentable. That explained why a lot of adults enjoyed watching the show and were able to watch it with their children. And by playing the music and featuring the artists on television, Dick gave rock 'n' roll a credibility it didn't get on radio.[1]

BROOKS

It became very advantageous for recording artists to appear on American Bandstand. If the kids liked your record, it stood a good chance of becoming a hit. So we had people like Bobby Darin, Connie Francis, Paul Anka, Jerry Lee Lewis, the Everly Brothers, and many more right from the start.
On our first network show we had an artist named Billy Williams as our featured guest. He had recorded "I'm Gonna Sit Right Down (and Write Myself a Letter)," and we wanted to enhance his

[1]From Dick Clark's American Bandstand, HarperCollins, 1997.

BROOKS (Cont'd)
number. So we placed him in front of a black
background, and I climbed up on top of a ladder
with a bag full of letters. They superimposed my
dropping letters in front of one camera over another
camera shot of Williams singing next to a mailbox.
As I grabbed a handful of letters, they slipped out of
my hands and this whole pile of letters appeared to
come flying down on top of Williams and the
mailbox. That was our first special effect on
network TV that didn't turn out so special.

By 1957, the rise of the youth culture and 12 million
teenagers made the music business stand up and take notice. The
industry began to listen to and cater to the young. The teens'
record of choice was the 45 rpm. Gone were the days of listening
to the large and awkward 78 rpm records in the family room. Now
teens bought the light and manageable 45s in their local record
shop, then played them at home on a portable record player in their
room after school or at night after homework.

DAVE APPELL
I remember going into a tailor shop and waiting for
the tailor to notice me. There he was, busy at his
workbench, watching American Bandstand on the
small TV, and keeping time to the music. It was
amazing how Dick Clark and the kids on his show
affected so many different types of people.

CLARK
Philadelphia was home to a lot of talented artists,
songwriters and producers. Critics who asked why
we used so many local acts didn't realize we were
booking ten acts a week on one show, and later five

CLARK (Cont'd)

acts a week on my Saturday night prime-time show from New York. That's fifteen artists a week. Often someone would cancel at the last minute. All we had to do was pick up the phone and call someone from South Philadelphia and they were at the studio quickly to fill in for someone who couldn't show up from California. The city was also home to a lot of people in the record business. These were the pioneer days of the modern recording industry, when the key word in the music business was "music" not "business." Record labels were small, independent companies often staffed by family members, friends, or a handful of employees. The people who started these companies were passionate about music. Our doors were always open to representatives from the record labels who wanted to convince us to play their latest releases or book their newest artists. Most of these people were honest, hard-working, and fun to be with. One such man was Red Schwartz who had been a popular DJ on WDAS-AM. After he became a record label promotion rep, I wouldn't always jump on his records. I was reluctant to play "Book of Love" by the Monotones because I thought it was a novelty song with limited appeal. One day Red took the unusual step of popping into my tiny office with the group in tow. He put the record on and had them lip sync to it, and I was finally convinced the song could be a hit, in fact, I said we'd put the group on the show that day. Then Red told me, "Dick, they're not the Monotones. They're five kids I picked up on the street and rehearsed for a day and a half." I did end up playing the song on the show, and Red was right — "Book of Love" was a top five hit in 1958.[1]

[1] From <u>Dick Clark's American Bandstand</u>, HarperCollins, 1997.

While it was true that many recording artists who appeared on American Bandstand were "larger than life," the real stars of the show were the dancers.

KLEIN

By 1959 we had a core group of about 35-40 regulars. They were all good dancers and more important, they were reliable kids. That was very important to us because we needed them to be there. That gave our show a continuity. At the height of their popularity they would get 15,000 fan letters a week, and were featured in teen magazines. We would get letters asking why were this boy and girl not dancing together? Did they have a fight? To this day I still get asked what became of them and who married whom.

BROOKS

At the height of their success, some of the regulars began to love the camera — a little too much. They developed this sixth sense as to where to be when the tally light went on. And they stayed there. When Dick saw them doing it, he'd tell them (over the loudspeaker) to move; they'd do it and then drift back again. So Ralph DiCocco (the other cameraman) and I would give Dick a helping hand. We'd move toward a specific couple that was hogging the camera. I'd come in from one side and Ralph from the other. Once past them, we'd close together. So they'd have to dance back, move out and around, or get squashed!

In 1958, two of the most popular couples on the show were Justine Carrelli and Bob Clayton, and Arlene Sullivan and Kenny Rossi.

SMITH

Justine and Bob were the dream couple. Justine would spend almost an hour on the bus ride each

SMITH (Cont'd)
day from her high school to the studio. Bob
Clayton watched the show from Delaware, fell in
love with Justine, made his way to the show and
asked her to dance. They became the most popular
and best-known couple on American Bandstand.
They personified the innocent lyrics of the songs
they danced to.

Arlene Sullivan and Kenny Rossi danced together on
American Bandstand for a little more than a year. At the height of
their popularity they received as many as 500 letters a day.

ARLENE SULLIVAN
My mother was a really big fan of the show and it
meant a lot to her. I think I began dancing on
Bandstand to get her attention. I never imagined
that I would become popular. As quiet and shy as I
was, I didn't think I would get noticed. When I
received my first fan letter I was shocked. And
when people asked me for my autograph, I was
surprised. I danced on a TV show and honestly felt
nothing I did was different from what kids were
doing at home in their basements. But maybe that's
why we were so popular. We were them and they
were us.

KENNY ROSSI
My mother watched the show during the Bob Horn
era and loved Jerry Blavat and Tom DeNoble.
When I got out of the eighth grade, my mother said
she wanted to see what I looked like on TV. I knew
how to dance. I was the only kid on my block that
had a dance party for his thirteenth birthday. So off
I went. My first day on the show, I sat in the stands.
The second day, this pretty dark-haired girl picked
me out of the bleachers. She actually pointed to me
and said, "Come here." That was Arlene. We

ROSSI (Cont'd)

started dancing together and the next week I was on
the Committee. At one point, I was getting about
2000-3000 fan letters a week. At Christmas time, I
would stuff these large duffel bags full of letters and
gifts to carry out of the studio. My parents had to
bring a station wagon to help me cart it all out of
there.

Rossi left the show in 1958 to pursue a recording career.
He studied voice in New York, and by the early 1960s was an
accomplished vocalist recording on Roulette and later Mercury
Records. His charted songs include "But I Do," "I'll Never Smile
Again," and "She Loves Me, She Loves Me Not." Rossi continued
to sing through the 1960s touring with "Dick Clark's Caravan of
Stars," and doing club and concert dates all over the country. He
ended his career in 1973 and went into private business.

By the end of the 1950s, American Bandstand was a huge
success with millions of viewers watching daily. By late 1960,
most of the popular dancers had grown older and left the show.
They were replaced by a new group of younger teens. In the early
1960s the show was still popular, but the network began to create
new programming. In October of 1962, ABC reduced Bandstand's
air time to 30 minutes. The following year, the show's daily run
came to an end.

Bandstand was moved to Saturday afternoon and shown
weekly. In early 1964, Dick Clark moved the show to California.

KLEIN
I think it was time. Dick had a lot of opportunities
out west and the show had run its course here.
WFIL was moving to a new studio on City Avenue.
I'm sure Roger Clipp was happy to be in a new
facility without a bunch of kids running up and
down the hallways.

ABC continued to air American Bandstand every Saturday
afternoon until 1987. From 1987 to 1989 it aired in syndication,
then went off the air, following a run of 32 years.

JOE FUSCO
The nicest thing to come out of my Bandstand days
were a lot of friendships that have endured over the
years. Lenny Natale and Betty Romantini have a
daughter who is my godchild. They're just an
example of the friends that are still an important
part of my life — people I met over 45 years ago on
American Bandstand. That was truly a wonderful
period in our lives that meant so much to so many
people. That could never happen again.

BANDSTAND COMMITTEE
(Partial List 1952-56)

Jerry Blavat	Andy Kamens
Tommy DeNoble	Marie DeLullo
Mary Ann Colella	Lucille Napoli
Peggy Scarlotti	Jan Murray
Kenny Newman	Len Cooney
Pete Stevens	Bill Young
Chuck Downey	Peggy Thompson
Blanche McCleary	Joe Sullivan
Bo Hockey	Ronald Kingsdorf
Billy Baretta	Juanita Gomez
Mickey Cullen	Adam Valleriano
Bobby Miluzzo	Joe Venutti
Joe Tati	Jim Wild
Jo Mazzu	*June Gamble
Monte D'Orcini	*Barbara Marcen
Jackie Chirico	*Bill Mulvhill
Johnny Little	*Carmella Raffa
Jerry Little	*Joanne MonteCarlo
Carol McCauley	*Anne Sullivan
Mary Lou Spencer	*Mike Montez
Ginny Callahan	*Jim Hudson
Pete Capobianco	*Terry Schreffler
Dave Feldbaum	*Pat Callahan
Dutchy Kramer	*Sid Paine
Cuz Bongiorno	*Bob Durkin
Bob Foley	*Frank Spagnuola
Earl Drake	*Bobbi Young
Mickey Duffy	*Rosemary Fergione
Lynn Baymer	*Rosemary Beltrante
Jackie Starr	*Nino Bambino
Bobby Devor	*Dottie Horner

*Also danced on American Bandstand.

AMERICAN BANDSTAND COMMITTEE
1957 - 1963
(Partial List)

Bob Clayton	Betty Romantini
Justine Carrelli	Mike Bolara
Arlene Sullivan	Frank Brancaccio
Kenny Rossi	Arlene DiPetro
Frankie Lobis	Bob DiPetro
Pat Molitierri	Joan Buck
Harvey Robbins	Jimmy Peatross
Barbara Levick	Carol Crossin
Carmen MonteCarlo	John Battaglia
Joe Fusco	Joyce Shaffer
Peggy Leonard	Norman Kerr
Carol Scaldeferri	Ed Kelly
Franny Giordano	Joanne Mataraza
Lenny Natale	Carol Higbee
Barbara Migilianis	Bunny Gibson
Lou DeSera	Terri Cieli
Charlie Zamil	Jim Russo
Joe Wissert	Carol Gibson
Billy Cook	Angel Kelly
Myrna Horowitz	Carol Hufnagel
Gary Levin	Larry Juliano
Bill Ettinger	Carol Smith
Walter Grzclak	Charlotte Russo
Ronnie Verbit	Angelo Vasaturo
Mary Ann Cuff	Marilyn Rudolph
Mary Beltrante	Lou Selino
Sue Beltrante	Carmen Jiminez
Frank Levins	Yvette Jiminez

AMERICAN BANDSTAND COMMITTEE
1957 - 1963
(Partial List)
(Continued)

Sandi Flynn
Monte Montez
Flossy Harvey
Marilyn Brown
Diane Celotto
Doris Olson
Paul Thomas
Barbara Warehol
Charles Hibib
Bobby Baratz
Richard Cartilage
Geri Iannetti
Patti Wavnett
George Wavnett
Ronald Joseph Caponegro

BILL HALEY, "the father of rock 'n' roll." (Courtesy of Temple University Urban Archives)

<u>BILL HALEY and ELVIS PRESLEY</u> in Cleveland in 1955. Elvis was a featured guest of Bill Haley and His Comets on a Midwestern tour. A few years later, the "father of rock 'n' roll" would hand over the reigns to the "king of rock 'n' roll." (Courtesy of the Comets)

<u>BILL HALEY and HIS COMETS</u> in 1955. Clockwise from top: Bill Haley, Dick Richards, Marshall Lytle, Joey Ambrose, Johnny Grande, and Billy Williamson. They opened the door for many groups to follow. (Courtesy of the Comets)

PETER FORD as a small boy with his mother, dancer **Eleanor Powell**, and father, actor **Glenn Ford** in Beverly Hills, California in the late 1940s. Ironically, it was "father and son" who helped lay a foundation for rock 'n' roll music in American pop culture. (Courtesy of Glenn Ford Library and Archives)

JOE GRADY and ED HURST in 1946. Their radio show (the 950 Club) was the first of its kind where an invited teenage audience would dance to music played on the air. (Courtesy of Ed Hurst)

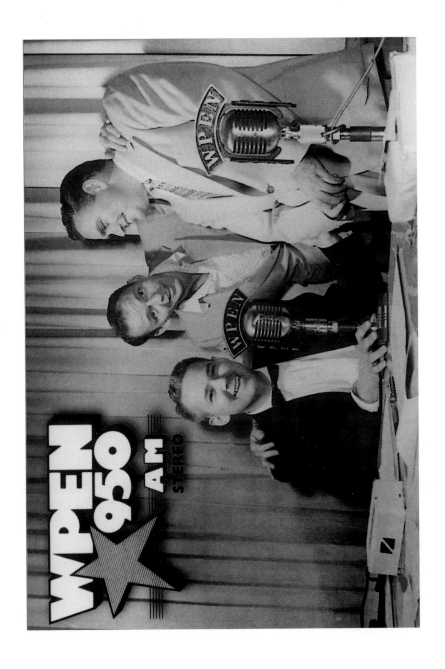

GRADY and HURST with 950 Club guest **FRANK SINATRA** in 1952. (Courtesy of Ed Hurst)

BOB HORN in 1953. He began as a popular radio personality, then established "Bandstand" as a local hit on television. (Courtesy of Temple University Urban Archives)

<u>BANDSTAND</u> in 1954. It aired weekdays in the afternoon and was successful from the very start. (Courtesy of Temple University Urban Archives)

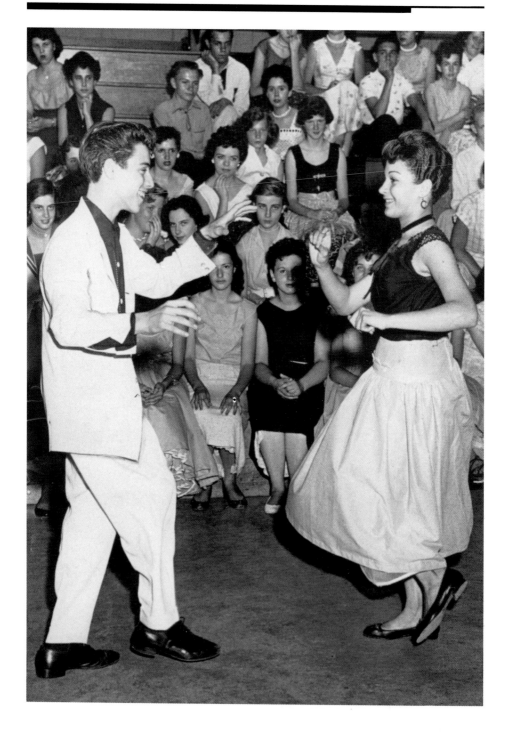

JERRY BLAVAT heats up the dance floor in 1955. He was head of the "Committee" and the top male dancer on the show. (Courtesy of Temple University Urban Archives)

<u>BOB HORN AND FAMILY</u> in June of 1956. (Courtesy of Temple University Urban Archives)

JERRY BLAVAT along with Peggy Scarlotti (extreme left), Mary Ann Colella (3rd from left holding the sign) and other committee members protest the removal of Bob Horn in June of 1956. (Courtesy of Temple University Urban Archives)

DICK CLARK as host of American Bandstand in 1958. He displayed a genuine rapport with the kids on the show. Together, they introduced the country to a new kind of music. (Courtesy of Temple University Urban Archives)

<u>RALPH EDWARDS, DICK CLARK and LEW KLEIN</u> on the set of "This Is Your Life" in Los Angeles in June of 1959. (Courtesy of Lew Klein)

ARLENE SULLIVAN with PAUL ANKA in 1959. She is fondly remembered by many "baby boomers," as part of a special time in their lives. (Courtesy of Arlene Sullivan)

KENNY ROSSI left American Bandstand at the height of his popularity to pursue a singing career. By the early 1960s, he had three charted hits and toured throughout the country. (Courtesy of Arlene Sullivan)

JUSTINE CARRELLI and BOB CLAYTON in 1958. They became the "dream couple" on American Bandstand. (Courtesy of Nino Bambino)

NINO BAMBINO and ROSIE BELTRANTE lead "the stroll" in 1958. (Courtesy of Dick Clark and Nino Bambino)

Teens wait to be admitted to WFIL Studios at 46th and Market Sts. in West
Philadelphia in 1959. (Courtesy of Temple University Urban Archives)

DICK CLARK displayed a unique talent of taking the rock 'n' roll music that America was afraid of, and broadcasting it to teens who loved it, while introducing it to adults who didn't. (Courtesy of Temple University Urban Archives)

AMERICAN BANDSTAND in 1959. Ray Smith: The show provided a home for many teens trying to find their place in an "age of conformity." (Courtesy of Temple University Urban Archives)

<u>LEE ANDREWS and the HEARTS</u> in 1957. They were one of the top R&B groups to emerge from Philadelphia in the late 1950s. (Courtesy of R&B Records)

DANNY and the JUNIORS in 1957. Left to right: Danny Rapp (lead), Joe Terranova (Terry), Dave White and Frank Maffei. (Courtesy of R&B Records)

The SENSATIONS first hit the charts in 1956. Yet their biggest seller came in 1962, when they recorded "Let Me In" written by lead singer Yvonne Baker. (Courtesy of R&B Records)

DAVE APPELL and the APPLEJACKS in the mid-1950s. Appell was a skilled guitarist and arranger who became the creative force at Cameo-Parkway Records. (Courtesy of Dave Appell)

The SILHOUETTES in 1957. Their recording of "Get A Job" is considered by many to be the "doo-wop" song of the 1950s. (Courtesy of R&B Records)

The TURBANS. Left to right: Charlie Williams, Andrew Jones, Mathew Platt, and Al Banks. They enjoyed success in the mid-1950s. (Courtesy of R&B Records)

THE MAJORS

<u>**The MAJORS**</u> created a distinctive sound, and in 1962 had their biggest success with "A Wonderful Dream." (Courtesy of R&B Records)

<u>CHARLIE GRACIE</u> at about age 12. His father gave him a choice: a new suit or a guitar. Guess which one he picked?

<u>CHARLIE GRACIE</u> in 1957. His three major hits in one year (Butterfly, 99 Ways and Fabulous) allowed Cameo Records to prosper. (Courtesy of Charlie Gracie Jr.)

<u>JAMES DARREN</u> in 1959. Handsome, multi-talented, and well-liked, he starred and co-starred in many feature films, television shows and became a recording star. In the mid-1980s he began directing network TV.

FRANKIE AVALON in 1962. He began as a skilled trumpet player before embarking on a recording career in 1957. He had over twenty charted hits between 1958 and 1962. (Courtesy of Temple University Urban Archives)

FRANKIE AVALON, musical arranger **RICHARD WESS** and **BOB MARCUCCI** in 1958. (Courtesy of Chancellor Entertainment)

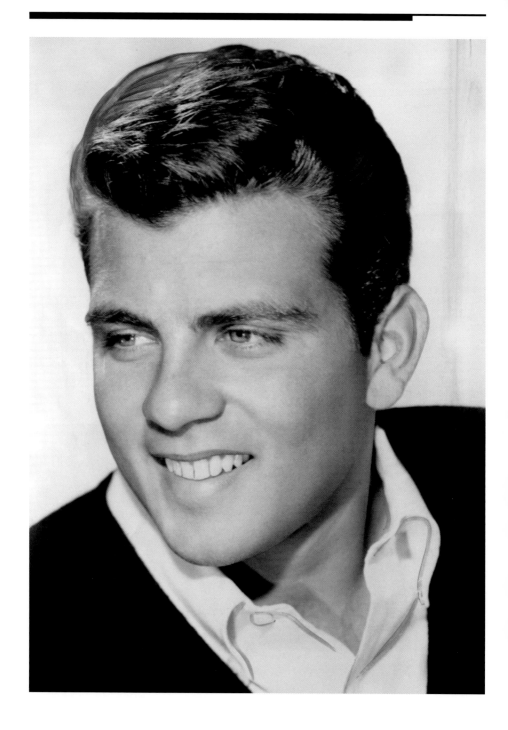

FABIAN in 1962. After recording ten charted hits in two years, he became a skilled actor, co-starred in thirty feature films and guest-starred on many network TV shows. (Courtesy of Temple University Urban Archives)

BOBBY RYDELL grew up as a musical talent who played drums, sang and did impersonations. He began his recording career in 1959 at age 17. By the early 1960s he was a major recording star. (Courtesy of J. Navary)

GRADY and HURST in 1958, about to inaugurate "Summertime on the Pier." The summer show would remain on the air for almost twenty years. (Courtesy of Ed Hurst)

<u>The **BLUE NOTES**</u> in the 1960s. In the 1970s they were known as HAROLD MELVIN and the BLUE NOTES, with Teddy Pendergrass singing lead. (Courtesy of R&B Records)

<u>CHUBBY CHECKER</u> gained worldwide fame with "the Twist" and became an innovator of several new dances in the 1960s. (Courtesy of Temple University Urban Archives)

SOLOMON BURKE

SOLOMON BURKE grew up with gospel music, and had over twenty charted hits on Atlantic Records. (Courtesy of R&B Records)

THE DOVELLS

The DOVELLS in 1961. Their memorable songs included "The Bristol Stomp" and "You Can't Sit down." (Courtesy of R&B Records)

DEE DEE SHARP became a teenage idol in 1962 thru her many appearances on American Bandstand.

THE ORLONS

The ORLONS in the early 1960s. They were unique in that every member of the group sang lead. (Courtesy of R&B Records)

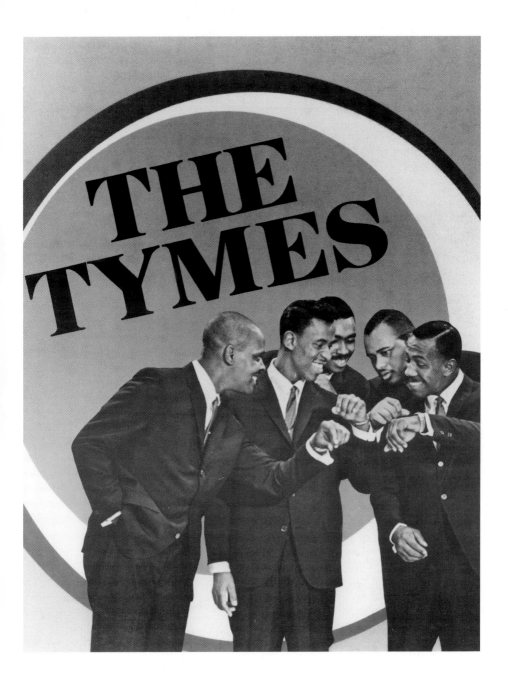

<u>The **TYMES**</u> in 1963. A month after they signed with Parkway Records, they recorded "So Much in Love" which became a number-one national hit, and one of the most popular ballads in music history. (Courtesy of R&B Records)

THE BLUEBELLES

<u>The **BLUEBELLES**</u> in 1962. They became known as PATTI LaBELLE and the BLUEBELLES, and had five charted hits within three years. In the early1970s they were a trio known as LABELLE. In 1977, Patti LaBelle launched a solo career. (Courtesy of R&B Records)

TAMMI TERRELL in the mid-1960s. Her classic duets with Marvin Gaye were some of the greatest love songs ever released on Motown.

THE INTRUDERS in 1968. They began as a "doo-wop" group in 1960, and later played a major role in the rise of "Philadelphia Soul."

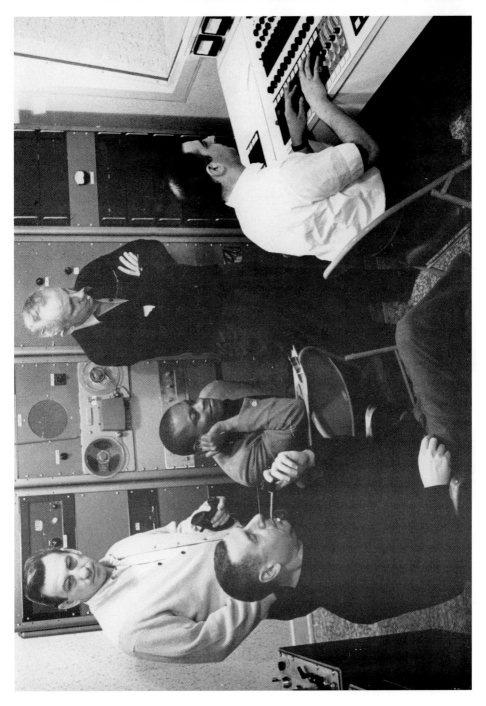

The CAMEO-PARKWAY production staff in 1964. Standing left to right: **DAVE APPELL** and **BERNIE LOWE**. Seated left to right: **KAL MANN**, **BILLY JACKSON**, and **JOE TARSIA** (at the console). (Courtesy of Temple University Urban Archives)

JOE NIAGARA with ELVIS PRESLEY on the set of the film "Blue Hawaii" in 1961. He became one of the top D.J.'s in Philadelphia on WIBG-AM and later spent many years on WPEN-AM. (Courtesy of Joe Niagara)

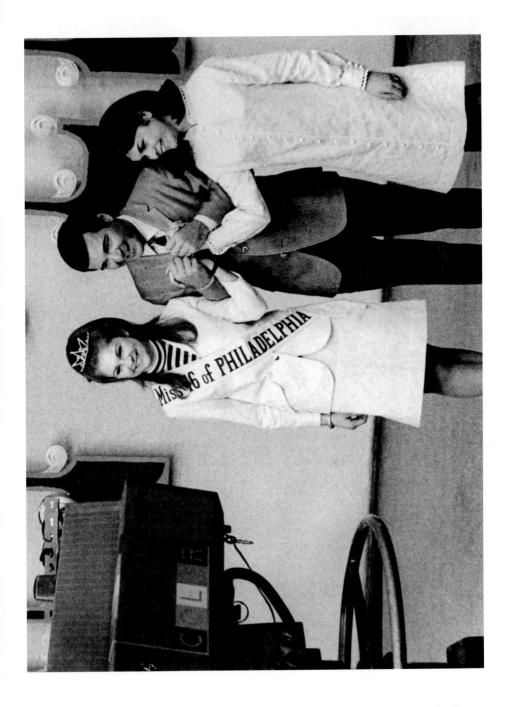

HY LIT on his television show in 1967. He became a premier rock 'n' roll D.J. who helped many recording artists of the time. (Courtesy of Temple University Urban Archives)

JERRY BLAVAT (The Geator with the Heater) has introduced several generations to his blend of commentary about the songs he plays on the air and the artists who performed them. (Courtesy of geatorgold.net)

JOCKO HENDERSON was said to have had "one of the most unique and pleasant voices in broadcasting history." (Courtesy of R&B Records)

GEORGIE WOODS became a renown D.J. on the Philadelphia airways and staged legendary rock shows at the Uptown Theater. (Courtesy of Temple University Urban Archives)

<u>GEORGIE WOODS</u> rescues a four-year-old child knocked down by a group of fans in North Philadelphia in 1964. Throughout a lengthy career in entertainment and community service, he improved, enhanced and inspired the lives of many. (Courtesy of Temple University Urban Archives)

LONG, LONG AND LONELY NIGHTS

In Southwest Philadelphia, near 49th and Woodland, lived a group of teens who were neighborhood friends and attended John Bartram High School. Arthur Lee Andrews, Rory and Wendell Calhoun, Butch Curry, and Ted Weems began singing in gospel groups before uniting as "The Dreams." Their wonderful harmony and extraordinary talent led to an audition with WHAT-AM D.J. Kae Williams, and in turn, Rainbow Records. The wife of the owner of Rainbow Records discovered a plastic heart on her desk, and accidentally found the name that became their signature.

In 1957 Lee Andrews and the Hearts recorded "Long, Long and Lonely Nights" on Mainline Records, and the song became a local hit. The record was later released on Chess Records in Chicago, and it rode to number 45 on the national charts.

Later that year came their second national hit: "Teardrops." In the spring of 1958, they signed with United Artists and recorded their third national hit: "Try the Impossible."

For many years after, Lee Andrews and the Hearts performed to sold-out audiences at Madison Square Garden, the Spectrum, Valley Forge Music Fair, and the Claridge Casino in Atlantic City. Today they are fondly remembered for their smooth, soulful and melodious harmony.

AT THE HOP

Another musical group from Southwest Philadelphia and John Bartram High School were the Juvenairs: Danny Rapp, Joe Terranova (Terry), Dave White, and Frank Maffei.

The Juvenairs, who began singing on street corners, were introduced to Artie Singer, a well-established musician and voice teacher in Philadelphia. Group member Dave White had written a song called "Let's All Do the Bop," which he and singer/song-writer Johnny Medora showed to Singer. Singer made a tape and brought it to Dick Clark, who liked the song but not the lyrics. He felt the bop was on the way out and suggested changing the title and lyrics.

ARTIE SINGER

I came out of the meeting with Dick Clark at 46th and Market and drove to WPEN at 21st and Walnut. In that space of time, I rewrote the whole song now centered around the hop, because every D.J. was doing hops. They didn't make the same kind of money at stations that they make today. When we got back into the studio, I put Danny Rapp on lead, and we renamed the group "Danny and the Juniors."

"At the Hop" was recorded in 13 takes in a studio at 13th and Market. The music was sparse — a piano, drums, and Singer on bass. He called his record label Singular, and gave the record number S711: "S" for Singer, and 7-11 because it was a crap shoot.

SINGER
I made 5000 copies. Disc Jockeys like Joe Niagara
and Hy Lit made it popular locally. But it took the
power of Dick Clark to send it off like a skyrocket
nationally.

Singer's Singular label didn't have the financial clout to
take the record nationally. So he leased the record to the newly
formed ABC-Paramount. Dick Clark had Danny and the Juniors
on American Bandstand in the fall of 1957. By December, "At the
Hop" was the No. 1 record in the country. It sold 2.5 million
copies, remained at the top for seven weeks, and sent the group on
tour.

Their follow-up "Rock and Roll Is Here to Stay" (also
written by Dave White) broke into the top 20 in March of 1958 and
became the anthem of the music business.

Another song by the group fondly remembered by many is
"Sometimes (When I'm All Alone)."

JOE TERRY
(DANNY AND THE JUNIORS)
"Sometimes (When I'm All Alone)" was the flip
side of "At the Hop" and charted by itself. It had a
wonderful 'a cappella' character, and to this day,
when we tour, musical groups will tell me this was
the one song that most influenced their style.

Singer co-wrote the next follow-up, "Dottie," that sold
moderately well. In 1961, the group switched labels. One of their
songs, "Twistin' USA" made it to No. 27, and "Pony Express" hit

the top 50. Over the next two-and-a-half years, the group recorded
five more charted hits. About this time, Dave White left the group.

In the 1970s, Danny and the Juniors were in public demand
once more.

TERRY

We toured the country and the success of films like
"American Graffiti," "Grease," and the TV series
"Happy Days" fostered our revival into the
mainstream. "At the Hop" became a big hit in
England and charted in the top 30.

In the early 1980s, lead singer Danny Rapp passed away.
Joe Terry took his place and kept the group going. Ironically, the
group enjoyed their greatest success in the 1980s doing over 200
concerts a year in every possible venue. Their latest CD, "For
Cool Grandkids Everywhere," received a top 50 Grammy Award
nomination.

THE IDOLS AND THE IDOLMAKER

Bob Marcucci grew up in South Philadelphia with ambition and curiosity about a larger world than the one he lived in.

After graduating from South Philadelphia High School, he began writing songs with his friend Peter DeAngelis. After shopping their demos to various record labels, Marcucci and DeAngelis decided to try their hand at producing, and they formed their own record company. Marcucci's brother managed the dining room at the Chancellor Hotel so they named their label Chancellor.

In early 1957, a 25-year-old Marcucci opened a record shop in a Philadelphia Farmers' Market. With a street-wise sense for promotion, he used the record shop in the open market to promote his newly-formed record company. He played the records, danced, and sang along with them, much to the delight of his customers.

Finally, the uncorked talent of Marcucci and DeAngelis struck lightning. They wrote and produced a song, "With All My Heart," recorded by Jodie Sands, which became a national hit. With the success of Jodie Sands, Marcucci decided to develop and manage talent along with promoting records that he and DeAngelis wrote and produced.

With his first success behind him, Marcucci began his search for new talent. Out of the hunt came two South Philadelphians: Frankie Avalon and Fabian Forte.

BOB MARCUCCI

I went to see a local band called "Rocco and the Saints." They were a dance band that played parish bazaars, weekend sock hops, and dances at teen clubs. I thought the lead singer was capable, but not the teenage idol type. I was about to leave when the sixteen-year-old trumpet player got up to sing. I took immediate notice. I thought he had all the ingredients. His name was Francis Avallone and he called himself Frankie Avalon. When I told him I wanted him to record, Frankie looked at me like I was "nuts," and said, "I'm not a singer. I'm a trumpet player." He had appeared on the "Jackie Gleason TV Show," and recorded an instrumental: "Trumpet Sorrento." I assured him he was much more than a trumpet player, and took him to the recording studio. He was young and raw but we took him to record hops and the reaction was unbelievable.

Avalon's first two songs, "Cupid," and "Teacher's Pet," were local hits aimed at teens. Marcucci and DeAngelis wrote "De De Dinah," and wanted Avalon to record it as his next single.

MARCUCCI

Before we recorded "De De Dinah," Frankie was joking and pinched his nose when he rehearsed the song. He also had a slight cold that day, but I thought the resulting sound was terrific. So I told him to go ahead and do it that way. Pete (DeAngelis) was fit to be tied. He didn't like it at all. But we only had one track, were done recording, and we had no money to go back and record again.

No one was sure what the reaction would be to the nasal version that Chancellor recorded in December of 1957. A week before its national release, Avalon sang the song on American Bandstand and "De De Dinah" soon sold close to a million copies.

His next three singles were aimed at teenage girls. "Gingerbread" sold nearly a million copies and "You Excite Me" about half that amount. Then Avalon recorded "Venus," a song written by Ed Marshall.

MARCUCCI
"Venus" was a departure from Frankie's previous recordings. Instead of a combo, we used an orchestra, with female vocals, bells and chimes over a soft calypso-type beat.

"Venus" was Avalon's biggest hit, selling more than a million copies in the spring of 1959. Three more million sellers followed: "Bobby Sox to Stockings," "Just Ask Your Heart," and "Why?" written by DeAngelis and Marcucci. Over a two year period, Avalon had seven songs in the top 10.

In the early 1960s, his acting career began to blossom. He co-starred with Alan Ladd in "Guns of the Timberland," with John Wayne in "The Alamo," and with Walter Pidgeon and Joan Fontaine in Irwin Allen's "Voyage to the Bottom of the Sea." In 1963, Avalon began to appear with Annette Funicello in a series of beach films that proved very popular.

In the mid 1960s, Avalon signed with United Artists and continued recording singles and albums. In the mid-1970s, a disco version of "Venus" was successful and in 1978, Avalon appeared in the musical "Grease," playing "Teen Angel" and singing "Beauty School Dropout."

In 1983, Avalon recorded his last single: "You're the Miracle." In the summer of 1985, he began touring with Fabian and Bobby Rydell as "The Golden Boys." The 50-city tour was a huge success, and continues to this day. In 1987 Avalon reunited with Annette Funicello for "Back to the Beach," a film parody of their earlier beach movies. Today, Avalon tours in "Grease," and continually makes concert and nightclub appearances. Two of his four sons, Frank and Tony, are accomplished musicians (playing drums and guitar, respectively) and accompany him on concert dates all over the world.

******

In the spring of 1958, while driving through his South Philadelphia neighborhood, Marcucci spotted an ambulance parked in front of the house of a close friend. He discovered that his friend's next door neighbor Dominic Forte had suffered a heart attack. It was then Marcucci first noticed Forte's 14 ½ year-old son, Fabian.

Marcucci would see Fabian again in the neighborhood and believed the youth was magnetic with potential star quality. One day, Marcucci approached him about representation. At first, young Forte was not interested in promises of teenage stardom.

Then he had a change of heart.

FABIAN FORTE

The only reason I agreed to give the record business
a try was to help my family. I had a father who was
disabled, my mother and two younger brothers. I
felt this might be an opportunity to help give them
what they needed.

With that in mind, Fabian jumped into the mix, undaunted

by the demands and pressures of a business that intimidated other

performers older and more experienced than he.

MARCUCCI

I never wavered in my belief that Fabian would
become a teenage idol. He listened, took direction,
worked extremely hard, and did what he was
supposed to do. Because of the success I had with
Frankie, I was able to get Fabian booked on
American Bandstand. Dick felt the same as I did,
and the reaction to Fabian was unreal.

Marcucci kept Fabian on the record hop circuit to help

build up a fan base. But the first two songs that DeAngelis and

Marcucci wrote for him didn't do well.

MARCUCCI

For some reason, Pete and I were unable to write
songs for him. Not the kind of hit records he really
needed. So we hired Doc Pumus and Mort Shuman,
who we felt were the appropriate songwriters, and
they came up with the song, "I'm a Man." I
arranged for Fabian to introduce the song on
American Bandstand in December of 1958, and we

MARCUCCI (Cont'd)
hit the charts two weeks later. Success was on the
way.

But the song that really launched him was "Turn Me

Loose," the Pumus-Shuman follow-up to "I'm a Man," in the

spring of 1959. That song went all the way to the top 10.

That year Chancellor's tandem of Frankie Avalon and

Fabian Forte was highly successful. Two of Avalon's releases

topped the charts, while three of Fabian's records made the top 10.

Fabian had ten charted hits in two years.

MARCUCCI
Frankie did well with the ballads while Fabian had
success with the rock 'n' roll tunes. It was a
balanced plan that worked to perfection.

With a successful recording career in tow, Fabian set his

sights on acting. He studied in New York with Wynn Handman,

and in Los Angeles with Sandy Meisner and Charles Conrad. He

appeared in 30 feature films and co-starred with actors such as

John Wayne, Stewart Granger, James Stewart, Maureen O'Hara,

Jack Palance, George Segal and Tuesday Weld. He also guest-

starred on network TV and won critical acclaim for his portrayal in

an episode of the ABC television series "Bus Stop" entitled "A

Lion Walks Among Us," directed by Robert Altman and shown

without commercial interruption.

FORTE
I really enjoyed being an actor. One of the more
gratifying things about making films was that we all

FORTE (Cont'd)

took acting seriously. It was a joy to be in that profession. I worked with a lot of great actors but my favorite was Jimmy Stewart. He was probably the most accessible of the superstars I worked with. He loved to rehearse and he cared about what everyone else was doing and how they felt. The two films I did with him were the happiest ones I ever worked on. Another nice thing about doing movies was you'd be on location in one spot for weeks or longer. That was a contrast to doing 45 one-nighters on tour in a bus like we did in the music industry. [2]

In addition to his nationwide tour with Frankie Avalon and Bobby Rydell, Fabian has produced his own concert series, "Fabian's Goodtime Rock 'n' Roll Show," featuring musical performers from the 1950s and 1960s. The series has aired on Public TV, in syndication, and pay-per-view.

In 1964, Marcucci, Avalon and Forte ended their professional association. The style of music was changing, and both Avalon and Forte were involved in their film careers.

In 1979 Marcucci began working as a technical advisor on a feature film called "The Idolmaker." The movie was based on his life and experience as mentor and manager. It was released in 1980. This experience led Marcucci to produce the remake of two classic 20th Century Fox films from the 1940s: "Razor's Edge"

[2] From the Tribune-Review, January 2004.

(released theatrically), and "A Letter to Three Wives" (an NBC MOW). Today Marcucci is still active (as President of Chancellor Entertainment) writing an autobiography and developing film projects.

****

Another South Philadelphian who took a somewhat different path and became a recording star was James Darren. As a teenager, he sang in nightclubs in Philadelphia and South Jersey.

JAMES DARREN
Music was a big part of our lives then. Most of the kids on my block all played musical instruments and there were lots of places to perform. My Dad would take me to clubs when I was a teenager, to listen to the music. I would get up and sing at Palumbo's, the CR Club, and the RDA Club. I'll never forget, one night we went to a bar called the White Elephant. They had a live sax player there, so I got up and sang. As I walked off stage, this man stopped me and said, "Here, kid, take this." I looked down and it was a five dollar bill. That was my first paying job as a professional!

In his late teens, Darren began to study drama with Stella Adler in New York, commuting twice a week via motorcycle. A photographer's assistant thought Darren had charisma and recommended him to legendary talent executive Joyce Selznick. This led to a seven-year contract with Columbia Pictures. Darren made 19 films while at Columbia beginning in 1956 with "Rumble on the Docks" (which premiered in Philadelphia at the Mastbaum Theater). In the film "Gidget," he played the role of Moondoggie, sang two songs, including the title tune, and became a major recording star. His next hit, "Goodbye, Cruel World," reached No. 1 on the charts and was nominated for a Grammy. His other top 10 entries included "Angel Face," "Conscience," and "Her Royal Majesty."

In the early 1960s Darren co-starred in a number of feature films and in 1966 starred in the ABC TV series "Time Tunnel." Throughout the 1970s he concentrated on singing and toured with comedian Buddy Hackett nationwide. He also guest-starred in many network TV shows, and in 1982 joined the cast of the long-running ABC series "T. J. Hooker." From the mid-1980s through the late 1990s he directed network television. In 1998, after his appearance as singer Vic Fontaine on "Star Trek: Deep Space Nine," he returned to singing. He has recorded for Concord Records and currently appears in concert throughout the country.

DARREN

People ask me what was it about South Philadelphia that gave rise to so many performers and entertainers. I can't say exactly. I would say South Philadelphia was unique in the sense that everyone not only knew each other, but looked out for and helped each other. It was an extremely tight-knit community with roots from Market Street to League Island Park, and from 25th Street to Front Street. You always got strong support from your friends and people in the neighborhood. And when someone became successful, it gave all of us inspiration.

CAMEO-PARKWAY

In the late 1950s through the early 1960s, Cameo-Parkway Records was probably the most productive and influential independent record company in the city of Philadelphia. The creative force behind the record label was musical arranger-producer Dave Appell and lyricist Kal Mann.

Appell had a varied career before collaborating with Kal Mann at Cameo-Parkway in 1958. He began arranging for big bands in the mid-1940s. In the 1950s he became musical director on the "Ernie Kovacs Show" in Philadelphia. Appell was also an accomplished guitarist and had his own group: "The Applejacks." In the late 1950s he had two national hits with the instrumentals "Mexican Hat Rock" and "Rocka-Conga." When Appell came to Cameo-Parkway, he was a jack-of-all-trades, doing background work, session work as a guitarist, engineering and arranging.

DAVE APPELL

Originally it was Cameo Records. Then it became Cameo-Parkway. Parkway was the budget line. In those days it was advantageous to have two labels. There were only so many releases you could put out on one label. With two, you were able to put out more product.

The creator and head of Cameo-Parkway was Bernie Lowe. Originally Lowe was a piano player with society bands in the 1930s. By the early 1940s, Lowe and fellow musician Artie Singer became members of the musical combo at the Walt Whitman Hotel in Camden, New Jersey. After the war, Lowe, with Singer's help, got a job with WIP Radio's studio orchestra. Lowe played accordion and piano while Singer played bass. When live orchestra on radio began to wane in the late 1940s, Lowe and Singer opened a vocal studio called Bern-Art. Lowe taught piano and Singer taught voice. As a result of the G.I. Bill, Lowe and Singer opened the 20th Century Institute of Music on Locust Street. Their administrator was Norman Black who was also the musical director of WFIL Radio. When he looked to fulfill musical needs for Paul Whiteman's TV Teen Club, Black hired Singer and Lowe. Singer became the bass player, Lowe played piano and eventually became musical director.

In the early 1950s, Kal Mann earned money by writing comedies, plays and parodies for big-name comedians and entertainment shows at resort hotels in the Poconos. He also lived across the street from the 20th Century Institute of Music. After taking piano lessons there, Mann approached Lowe and Singer with lyrics he had written. Mann and Singer began to collaborate.

SINGER

We wrote a song called "I Really Can't Stop Loving You." It did well down south and began to catch on in other regional areas. Then Doris Day released a similar title which made the promotion of our song very difficult. Eventually it died.

With no more success in sight, Singer parted amicably with Lowe and Mann.

In late 1956, Lowe formed Cameo Records but was unsuccessful. Broke and operating out of his basement, Lowe picked Charlie Gracie, a South Philadelphia singer-guitarist, whom he had watched on TV Teen Club (and who had been recording on the Cadillac and Twentieth Century Record labels) to record "Butterfly," a song that he and Kal Mann had written.

CHARLIE GRACIE

Bernie was able to record the song by giving Emil Corson, the owner of a local recording studio, a percentage of it in return for studio time. The record cost about $600.00 to make. Bernie was a musical genius. Once he got into the studio he worked with precision. He knew exactly what kind of sound he wanted from the artist, engineer and everyone involved.

Soon after its release, Lowe took the song to Dick Clark who liked it. Once it played on American Bandstand, it began to catch on nationally. "Butterfly" became a worldwide hit, and was one of the biggest sellers in 1957. With the success of "Butterfly," the flip side "99 Ways," and Gracie's follow-up, "Fabulous," Cameo Records began to prosper.

GRACIE

The early rock 'n' roll music was all about the backbeat and melody. The lyrics were almost incidental in my opinion. The only true lyricist at that time was Chuck Berry. To me he was the great poet of rock 'n' roll because his lyrics told a story.

GRACIE (Cont'd)

In the early days, rock 'n' roll was great dance music with a fresh sound. That's because we recorded it live, unlike today, and we'd do take after take until we got it right. We had no one to emulate. We started it all. Our music was the bottom of the pyramid of everything that was to follow. We set the trend of what was to come and last to this day.

JAMES DARREN

What's interesting is that early rock 'n' roll and R&B music from the '50s and early '60s is still going strong. You have a music with simple lyrics, basic chords and harmony, that's lasted for 50 years. It's still played all over the country, not just by people who discovered it, but by today's young people as well.

JOE TERRY

I don't think that any other form of music reaches as many people of different age groups as the good old rock 'n' roll music from the '50s and '60s. I base that on what I see at festivals and concerts throughout the country. It seems that rock 'n' roll music has maintained its popularity with a mass audience and a more diverse one than any other musical form.

With Gracie's success, Bernie Lowe began to look for his next recording star.

Bobby Rydell grew up in the same Italian neighborhood as James Darren, Frankie Avalon and Fabian. As a small child he would sit in front of the TV set and impersonate performers like Milton Berle, Louis Prima, and Johnnie Ray.

BOBBY RYDELL

When I was about 5 or 6, my dad would take me to
the Earle Theater at 11th and Market. We'd go in
the afternoon to see big bands like Benny
Goodman. When I saw Gene Krupa playing drums,
I told my father that's what I wanted to do.

At about 7 or 8, Rydell and his father would continually go
to places like the Erie Social Club, BR Club and RDA Club, to
listen to the bands. It was there that young Rydell got up to sing
and do impersonations. At age 10, he auditioned for Skipper
Dawes of the Paul Whiteman TV Teen Club Show.

RYDELL

There was a record that Sammy Davis had put out.
It had singers doing actors on one side and actors
doing singers on the other. I did singers doing
actors like Humphrey Bogart and James Cagney.
Skipper liked what I did and I became a regular on
the show for about three years.

When Rydell was in his early teens, he was asked to pinch-
hit for drummer Chippy Peters in a band called "Rocco and the
Saints" (Frankie Avalon played trumpet). The group was
performing at Bay Shores in Somers Point, NJ. Rydell stepped in
and also sang and did impersonations.

A bass player named Frankie Day (with a group called Bill
Duke and the Dukes) became interested in Rydell's talent, and after
permission from Rydell's father and a handshake agreement, took
the teenage Rydell to various recording studios. No one seemed
interested in the wake of Frankie Avalon, Fabian, and Paul Anka.

But when they went to Cameo Records, Bernie Lowe remembered Rydell from Paul Whiteman's TV Teen Club (where Lowe played the piano), and he signed Rydell to a contract.

Rydell's first three records did not fare well. Then Lowe came up with "Kissin' Time." The record caught on in Philly, Detroit, Boston, and Cleveland. Dick Clark played it on American Bandstand, and within three weeks it became a national hit. "We Got Love" was a solid follow-up and peaked in the top 10.

RYDELL
I remember recording "We Got Love" in BellSound Studios in New York City. Bernie didn't like the bass sound and we went into the studio three days in a row to get what he wanted. When he listened to it all, I believe he finally took the second take from the first day.

In early 1960, Rydell had his biggest selling single, "Wild One," which became his first million seller.

ED HURST
When I sold George Hamid (the owner of Steel Pier) on the idea of doing a show there, we needed promotion. So Joe and I went to Bobby Rydell and Bernie Lowe, and Bernie put out a one-sided 45 called "Steel Pier," recorded by Bobby. So we said on the air, "If you send in 25 cents, we'll send you the record." Well, old man Hamid went out of his mind because he knew the response we'd get. He said, "Ed, take that off the air. We're not gonna do that." I said, "Mr. Hamid, we can't. Once you make an offer, you can't take it back." Well, we got over 50,000 quarters in the mail, and Hamid had to

HURST (Cont'd)
hire about eight girls to send out the 50,000 records
of Bobby Rydell singing "Steel Pier."

Over the next three years, Rydell enjoyed a string of hits
that sold more than half a million copies each. Several, including
"Good Time Baby," "I've Got Bonnie," "I'll Never Dance Again,"
and "Wildwood Days," made the top 20. "Volare" was his second
million seller, and in 1963 "Forget Him" sold over a million copies
as well. That same year Rydell appeared opposite Ann-Margret in
the film version of the hit Broadway musical, "Bye Bye, Birdie."
He later recorded for Capitol Records, and in the 1970s moved into
the "pop area."

In the 1980s, Rydell began touring with Frankie Avalon
and Fabian, and in the 1990s he appeared in "big-band style"
concert dates and on a number of TV specials.

RYDELL
I was always a fan of big band and jazz and
although I made a career of doing rock 'n' roll, if I
had my choice, I would have been a big-band
singer. One of my greatest joys was doing an album
called "An Era Reborn," where I saluted the big
bands in the style of Artie Shaw, Benny Goodman,
and Tex Beneke. I also did another album, "Bobby
Salutes the Great Ones," where I did the songs of
Crosby and Jolson. Dave Appell put it together and
he was marvelous on the charts.

****

In 1959, Kal Mann was introduced to 18-year-old Ernest Evans from South Philadelphia. Evans had worked at a poultry shop after school where he entertained customers with singing, humor and imitations. Henry Colt (the shop owner) was impressed by his talent and introduced Evans to Mann.

Evans began to frequent the Cameo-Parkway Studio where he sang and did imitations of recording artists like Fats Domino whom he greatly admired. Evans had been given the nickname Chubby by his first employer, but during a chance meeting with the Dick Clarks, it was Clark's wife who re-christened him "Chubby Checker," a sly reference to Fats Domino.

Finally given the chance to record for Parkway, Checker's first record was "The Class," where he did singing impersonations. The recording was a modest hit, but it was the record he released a year later, in the summer of 1960, that made him a worldwide success.

APPELL

We heard a song called "The Twist" that was
recorded a year before by Hank Ballard. It got
some play with the jukebox crowd and became a
R&B hit, but never crossed over to the "pop" charts.
But we liked it and decided to do it with Chubby.
We thought it would be a good way to get him on
Bandstand. He was 19 and fresh at that point.
Hank Ballard was already in his thirties, and
considered an "old man" by Bandstand standards.

While Ballard had a hard-driving rhythmic style, Checker was more cheerful, celebrating and happy-go-lucky, downplaying the sexual and suggestive. "The Twist" was a simple dance to do, where you moved your hips and feet in a twisting motion. Teenagers and young adults caught on quickly and "The Twist" became a dance sensation.

Checker recorded two more dance hits: "The Hully Gully," and "Pony Time." But Appell and Mann weren't done with "The Twist." They knew this was no novelty. So they wrote, "Let's Twist Again" in the spring of 1961, and that proved as popular as the original.

APPELL

With the huge success of "The Twist," Bernie decided to re-issue the original recording that November, and it topped the charts again. It had two stops at the top more than a year apart. "The Twist" was a number one hit in 1960 and again in 1961.

In the early 1960s, Cameo-Parkway was highly prolific and profitable with Bobby Rydell, Chubby Checker, Dee Dee Sharp ("Mashed Potato Time"), the Dovells ("Bristol Stomp," "You Can't Sit Down"), the Orlons ("South Street," "Wah Watusi") and the Tymes ("So Much In Love"). In one year there were almost 20 charted hits in the top 40.

DEE DEE SHARP

I grew up with gospel music and studied the classics from age 4 to 21, but never got involved in the rock 'n' roll dances. So when I was to appear on

SHARP (Cont'd)

American Bandstand to sing "Mashed Potato Time," I didn't know how to do the dance. My brother taught me how to do it, or more honestly, how to fake it, and the result is, I've been faking it all these years!

MARK STEVENS
(THE DOVELLS)

By the 1960s we had formula production with people like Dave Appell and Kal Mann, writing songs with the same thread and fiber running through it. That became the Cameo-Parkway sound. With Motown, you had Holland, Dozier, Holland writing many of the hits that composed a formula that became the Motown sound. Then you had the Beach Boys in the early '60s with a West Coast sound that also became very formulated. The difference being, out west you had arrangers who were brought into the studio to "sweeten" the sound and make it more precise, the same way they did with many motion picture and television shows; even from the conception of the rhythm section (guitar, bass, keyboard, drums), which built the track. Those parts were already written and you played them as written. The east coast sound was more soulful and immediate in feeling. We improvised and felt the song before it was laid down. We gave the musicians a chance to bring something to the table.

AL "CAESAR" BERRY
(THE TYMES)

We had two studio musicians: a drummer named Bernard Purdy, and a guitarist named Eric Gale who played on all our sessions. They would play through what was on the charts, then put them down

BERRY (Cont'd)
and add their "feel and personality" to them. That
gave our music its own signature.

END OF AN ERA

In 1964, the record business began to change rapidly. British rock groups began to take over. Their records climbed quickly up the charts and they were predominant on the air.

The British Invasion and American Bandstand's departure signaled the end of Cameo-Parkway. In 1964, Chubby Checker was the only artist to have a top 40 charted hit. The company lost heavily and in 1965, Lowe sold his controlling interest to a group of investors. Two years later, the company was sold again. The music focus had shifted to the English artists and to Motown in Detroit.

Gone was doo-wop where group harmony pervaded, and the style of R&B as we knew it in the late '50s and early '60s.

DICK RICHARDS
The rhythmic accents of the drum and bass became more prevalent. By the mid-1960s, the guitar, bass, keyboard and drums took over. The sax and trumpet were reduced to minor status, if any. While we played a kind of "swing rock," the music that came after us was more of a "funk rock" with a fuller sound.

JERRY BLAVAT
With the end of the doo-wop era, it became very difficult for recording artists in this country to get air time. The radio stations began playing everything British. Over 60 percent of the playlist were the Beatles, Rolling Stones, Dave Clark Five,

BLAVAT (Cont'd)
Jerry and the Pacemakers, Freddy and the
Dreamers, Herman's Hermits, Chad and Jeremy,
etc.

JOE NIAGARA
(D.J.: WIBG-AM; HOST: WPEN-AM)
Yet some of the English stuff was good, especially
the Beatles, once you got past their initial period.
Songs like "Yesterday" and "Something in the Way
She Moves" attracted pop singers like Sinatra. He
recorded three different versions of the latter. In
one take he spent over five minutes on the
presentation. That shows how much he thought of
the song.

Aside from the British, a standout figure in the music
industry was Berry Gordy Jr., who established Motown Records.
With a staff of songwriters, producers and musicians, Motown
built one of the most impressive rosters of artists in pop music
history. The cast included: Martha Reeves and the Vandellas,
Smokey Robinson (also a hit songwriter) and the Miracles, Mary
Wells, Marvelettes, Four Tops, Temptations, Supremes, Stevie
Wonder, Marvin Gaye and Tammi Terrell. They were backed by a
group of studio musicians known as the Funk Brothers, who
shaped the Motown sound and included: Joe Hunter, Earl Van
Dyke, and Johnny Griffith (bass), Robert White, Joe Messina and
Eddie Willis (guitar), James Jamerson and Bob Babbitt (bass)
Benny Benjamin, Richard "Pistol" Allen, and Uriel Jones (drums),
Jack Ashford (percussion and vibes), Herbie Williams (trumpet),
Hank Crosby (sax) and Paul Riser (trombone).

NIAGARA

If you look at the Motown music of the mid-1960s, you sense it was a more refined take on what the kids were looking for. The sound was a bit more elaborate and polished. It attracted an older listening audience as well. Prior to that, you dealt with teens. Now you had 21-year-olds and older listening to the Supremes, Temptations, and Smokey Robinson, and saying, "Hey, that's a good record." They weren't necessarily saying that about the earlier doo-wop and R&B music. It was the teenage audience who was drawn to that.

RAY SMITH

Much of the rock music began to take on a whole different character by the mid-to-late-1960s. By the time the Beatles came on the scene, many of the teenagers that were there for the birth of rock 'n' roll were college-age and their interests were entirely different. The drug culture and anti-war movement became dominant themes. This was reflected by songs like "Sgt. Pepper's Lonely Heart Club Band," "Eve of Destruction," "Lucy in the Sky with Diamonds," "Mellow Yellow" and so on. The cultural change had a profound effect on music. Some of the R&B sound was connected to the political time as well. Aretha Franklin's "Respect" hit at the same time as the Detroit riots and became a watch-cry for young blacks. So where the '50s and early '60s doo-wop and R&B was fun and melodic, much of the mid-to-late '60s music was socially conscious and internalized.

STEVENS

The late '50s and early '60s was a special time for us. Coming out of Overbrook High School, we grew up in an R&B era, in a mixed group atmosphere with no division. It was all about the

STEVENS (Cont'd)

music. At the Uptown Theater we saw James
Brown and the Original Flames, Smokey Robinson
and the Original Miracles, Hank Ballard and the
Midnighters. We watched in awe at the energy and
soulfulness of these performers, the music they
played, and the way they performed it. Everything
about the production was awe-inspiring. Then we
would go home and try to emulate it. And it wasn't
just us. Phil Spector produced one of the finest
R&B records of all time: "You've Lost That Lovin'
Feeling" by the Righteous Brothers. Where do you
think that came from? And it didn't stop there. The
creation of Blue-Eyed Soul in the 1970s with
Philadelphians like Hall and Oates originated from
the same source.

STEPHEN CALDWELL
(THE ORLONS)

It was about our expression of the music. That was
our number one priority. We had two auditions at
Cameo-Parkway which gave everyone in our group
the chance to sing lead. It was there we
demonstrated how much the music meant to us.
That was what led to our contract and a wonderful
music career.

BERRY

Back then, Cameo-Parkway was like Motown. We
had in-house artists that would back up other artists
such as Chubby Checker and Dee Dee Sharp. It was
a big happy family and everyone did what was
expected of them. We went from singing on the
street corner to the big-time. So it didn't matter to
us where we fit in. Just being part of the musical
process was a true sense of joy to all of us.

SHARP

I feel very fortunate to have had a career in rock 'n'
roll when the music was young, fresh, and I
sampled everything. Cameo-Parkway was a
wonderful family. Everyone loved what they did
and truly helped each other. Those years were a
great experience for all of us: the performers as well
as the people who loved listening to the music!

By the mid-1960s, for the first time in many years, there
was quiet in Philadelphia — the city of music. By the late 1960s
and early 1970s, music again began to proliferate in the Quaker
City with the creative duo of Kenny Gamble and Leon Huff in the
era of "Philly Soul." A new sound was provided by Eddie
Holman, the Intruders, Delfonics, Stylistics, O'Jays, and Harold
Melvin and the Bluenotes. But there are those who will never
forget the rich harmony and fundamental backbeat of the doo-wop
and R&B music of the early rock 'n' roll years. That remains a
cherished piece of time in the hearts of many people.

THE ORIGINAL COMETS

The COMETS on tour and still "rockin' around the clock." (Courtesy of the Comets)

CHARLIE GRACIE
International Recording Star

CHARLIE GRACIE performs on the east coast and every year plays to large crowds in the U.K. and Europe. His latest CD ("I'm All Right") is on Lanark Records. (Courtesy of Charlie Gracie Jr.)

Photo: Michael Hiller

JAMES DARREN returned to singing in 1999, recording for Concord Records and appearing in concert. His most recent CD ("Because of You") is a tribute to many of our best-remembered pop vocalists. (Courtesy of Concord Records)

<u>FRANKIE AVALON</u> performs in concert with sons **Tony** (on guitar) and **Frank** (on drums) in Las Vegas in the spring of 2004. The Avalons have entertained audiences worldwide.

FABIAN appears in concert with Frankie Avalon and Bobby Rydell, and also produces his own concert series of musical performers from the 1950s and 60s. (Courtesy of Oscar Arslanian Management)

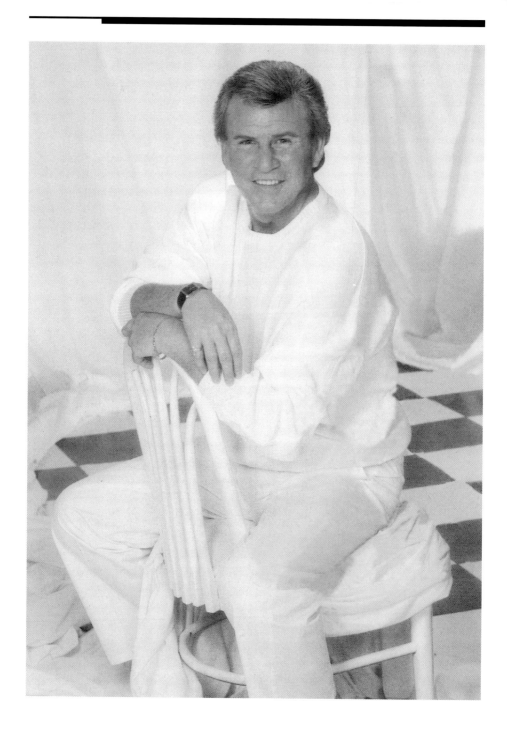

BOBBY RYDELL performs today blending pop and past hits with a still-vibrant voice reminiscent of his earlier years. (Courtesy of the Rydell Family)

<u>BOB MARCUCCI</u> is currently writing an autobiography and developing film projects for Chancellor Entertainment. (Courtesy of Chancellor Entertainment)

<u>DEE DEE SHARP'S</u> current repertoire includes contemporary R&B, jazz, and pop hits in addition to her rock and soul favorites. (Courtesy of Dee Dee Sharp)

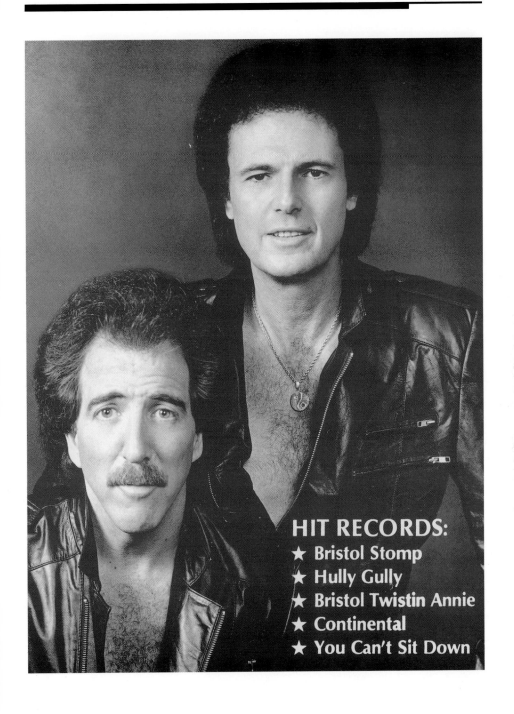

HIT RECORDS:
★ Bristol Stomp
★ Hully Gully
★ Bristol Twistin Annie
★ Continental
★ You Can't Sit Down

<u>The **DOVELLS**</u> with original members **MARK STEVENS** and **JERRY GROSS**. Their current concert act is a skillful mix of music and comedy. (Courtesy of Jerry Gross)

The DOVELLS perform on the Clinton campaign trail in 1992.

The ORLONS. Original member Stephen Caldwell leads a revised group that performs nationwide blending their hits with others of the era. (Courtesy of the Orlons)

Photo Credit: Keith Major

<u>PATTI LaBELLE</u> continues to enjoy a long-lasting career in contemporary music. (Courtesy of Aliya Crawford and W&W Public Relations)

DANNY and the JUNIORS with original members **JOE TERRY** (lead singer) and **FRANK MAFFEI**. The third member is **BOB MAFFEI**. They appear nationwide. (Courtesy of Frank Maffei)

The TYMES today. **NORMAN BURNETT, LAFAYETTE GAMBLE, DONALD BANKS, JIMMY WELLS** and **AL "CAESAR" BERRY**, bring joy to countless fans throughout the country, blending pop and soul hits from the 60s and 70s. (Courtesy of Al "Caesar" Berry)

<u>DICK RICHARDS</u> (of BILLY HALEY and HIS COMETS) on stage at the People's Light and Theater Company in 1984. He became an accomplished actor who appeared on Broadway, in feature films and on network television.

PETER FORD in May of 2004. Fifty years before, as a 9-year-old boy growing up in Beverly Hills, California, he played a small but pivotal role in launching a musical revolution. (Photo by Linda Ford)

POP, ROCK AND R&B ARTISTS

FROM

PHILADELPHIA

AND THE

DELAWARE VALLEY AREA

Marian Anderson

She was a world-renown contralto with a rich and beautiful voice, who sang both opera and spirituals.

She gave her first concert at New York's Town Hall at the age of 27. After studying in London, she performed extensively in Europe for ten years. She returned to the U.S. in 1935 and became the country's third highest concert box office draw.

In 1939 she was denied a concert engagement by a Washington, D.C. organization which created a national protest. In support of her, First Lady Eleanor Roosevelt and the U.S. Department of the Interior arranged for her to sing at the Lincoln Memorial. Her concert drew 75,000 people and a radio audience of millions.

In 1955, at the age of 57, she made her debut with the Metropolitan Opera Company, and became a permanent member.

With a combination of dignity, serenity, talent and perseverance, she passed on a legacy of accomplishments for many artists to live up to.

Lee Andrews and the Hearts
(Lee Andrews-lead, Rory Calhoun, Wendell Calhoun, Butch Curry and Ted Weems)

The group first got together at John Bartram High School in Southwest Philadelphia in the early 1950s. They were discovered singing locally, and signed with Mainline Records. Their first local hit was *Long, Long and Lonely Nights*, which was later sold to Chess Records and peaked at No. 45 on the national charts. *Tear Drops* was their second national hit, released later that year. In 1958 they recorded *Try the Impossible* for United Artists, which became their third national hit. One of the most successful R&B groups to come out of Philadelphia in the late 1950s.

Frankie Avalon

Born in South Philadelphia and tutored on the trumpet by his father, he performed on local and national TV. Discovered at age 16, he launched a singing career in 1957. He had over 20 charted hits from 1958 to 1962 on Chancellor Records. They include: *De De Dinah, You Excite Me, Gingerbread, I'll Wait for You, Bobby Sox to Stockings, Why, Venus, A Boy Without a Girl, Just Ask Your Heart, Two Fools, Swingin' on a Rainbow, Don't Throw Away All Those Teardrops, Where Are You, Togetherness, A Perfect Love, All of Everything, Who Else but You, True True Love, You Are Mine, Tuxedo Junction* and *A Miracle.*

He began a film career in the early 1960s. His credits include: *Guns of the Timberland, The Alamo, Voyage to the Bottom of the Sea, Drums of Africa, The Castilian, Beach Party, Muscle Beach Party, Bikini Beach, Beach Blanket Bingo, I'll Take Sweden, Fireball 500, The Jet Set, Horror House, The Take, The Hunters, Grease, Back to the Beach* and *Troop Beverly Hills.*

Network TV appearances include: *A Dream is a Wish Your Heart Makes — The Annette Funicello Story, Sabrina, The Teenage Witch, Full House, Burke's Law, Happy Days, Fantasy*

Island, The Love Boat, Police Story, Love - American Style, It Takes a Thief, The Patty Duke Show, the Eleventh Hour and *Rawhide.* He currently tours in the musical *Grease* and appears in concert throughout the country.

Thom Bell

He became known for his impeccable arrangements and, along with Kenny Gamble and Leon Huff, was a principal architect of the *Philly Soul Sound.* As a youth, he studied classical piano and joined Gamble's harmony group, "The Romeos," in 1959.

At 19 he worked as a conductor and arranger for Chubby Checker. In the late 1960s, he produced such classics by the Delfonics as *La La Means I Love You* and *Didn't I Blow Your Mind This Time.*

Reunited with Gamble and Huff, he became involved with releases such a Jerry Butler's *Only the Strong Survive,* Billy Paul's *Me and Mrs. Jones,* Harold Melvin and the Blue Notes' *If You Don't Know Me by Now*, and the O'Jay's *Love Train.*

In the mid '70s, Bell produced for Johnny Mathis and the Spinners; in the '80s, he did two albums for Deniece Williams; and in the '90s did session work with James Ingram and Earth, Wind and Fire.

Jerry Blavat

He began his musical kinship as the top male dancer on Bob Horn's Bandstand from 1953-1956. After graduating from high school in 1958, he began promoting records for Cameo-Parkway and was road manager for Danny and the Juniors.

In 1960, Blavat got into radio by an act of bravado. The owner of the Venus Lounge bet the Geator with the Heater he could not do a radio show from his nightclub. So Blavat went to WCAM in Camden and purchased an hour of radio time. With the acquired radio time, Blavat was allowed to resell commercials within it, which he did to pay for the air time. When a severe snowstorm closed the club, and the city too, Blavat made his way to Camden, determined to air those commercials, and armed with an assortment of Chuck Berry, Fats Domino and Little Richard records few teens had heard at the time. The storm that immobilized the listeners also immobilized the Geator's replacements at the station. His one hour of evening radio time turned into all night.

Unlike other D.J.s, Blavat would do informative commentary on the music he played and the artists who performed it. Listeners didn't know what was better: his patter or his platters. He continued the frenetic pace until the morning D.J. showed up at 6 A.M. By then the verdict was in. Blavat was a huge hit and began a career that has never lost momentum.

In addition to his radio and TV work over the past 44 years, "the boss with the hot sauce" has appeared at dances, clubs and events all over the Delaware Valley and "down the shore," (including his summer residence at "Memories") introducing several generations to the sound he's made the musical signature of Philadelphia.

The Bluebelles
(Patti LaBelle, Sarah Dash, Cindy Birdsong, and Nona Hendryx)

The group scored their first big hit in 1962 with *I Sold My Heart to the Junkman.* Patti LaBelle became lead singer and the group became Patti LaBelle and the Bluebelles. Several top 40 singles followed: *Down the Aisle* and *You'll Never Walk Alone* for Parkway. In the mid-1960s, the group had two more charted hits with *All or Nothing* and *Take Me for a Little While*, both on Atlantic Records.

Cindy Birdsong left the group in 1967 to join the Supremes. In the 1970s as a trio, the group became known as LaBelle. In 1977 Patti LaBelle launched a solo career.

The Blue Notes
(Teddy Pendergrass, Harold Melvin, Bernard Wilson, Lawrence Brown, Lloyd Parks)

In 1954, Harold Melvin formed a quintet called the Blue Notes. In 1960, they recorded *My Hero* which became a national hit. In the mid-1960s they hit the charts again with *Get Out (and Let Me Cry)*. In the early 1970s the group was called Harold Melvin and the Blue Notes. (Harold did not sing lead, but managed the group and sang with them. Teddy Pendergrass was the lead.)

With the renown team of Kenny Gamble and Leon Huff producing them, their hits include *If You Don't Know Me by Now, The Love I Lost, Bad Luck, Where Are My Friends,* and *Wake Up Everybody.*

Timmy Brown

He became an all-pro running back in the 1960s NFL with the Philadelphia Eagles, but his heart was in music.

As a child growing up in an Indiana orphanage, he studied voice and tap. In college he formed his own band and performed at clubs and dances.

In the early '60s, in Philadelphia, he studied voice with Artie Singer and recorded for the Singular and Mercury labels. After releases of *Running Late* and *If I Loved You*, he scored with *I've Got a Secret* which rose on the local charts.

He later turned to acting and appeared in such feature films as *Mash* and *Nashville.* On TV he played the role of *Spearchucker* in the early years of *Mash*, and was a regular on the soap opera *Capitol.* He also guest-starred in *T.J. Hooker, Nell, The Mary Tyler Moore Show, Adam-12, Cades County,* and *The Wild, Wild West.*

Solomon Burke

He grew up singing gospel and in his teens had his own church, from which he broadcast a weekly radio show. Eventually he signed with Atlantic Records, and a decade later with MGM. His biggest success came in the 1960s. His charted hits include: *Just Out of Reach, Cry to Me, Down in the Valley, I Really Don't Want to Know, If You Need Me, Can't Nobody Love You, You're Good for Me, He'll Have to Go, Goodbye Baby, Everybody Needs Somebody to Love, Yes I Do, The Price, Got to Get You off My Mind, Tonight's the Night, Someone is Watching, Only Love, Baby Come on Home, I Feel a Sin Coming On, Keep a Light in the Window Till I Come Home, Take Me, I Wish I Knew,* and *Proud Mary.*

Chubby Checker

He was introduced to Kal Mann of Parkway Records as a teenager. His first record was *The Class*, composed of singing impersonations, in the summer of 1959. His next recording, *The Twist*, released a year later, brought him worldwide fame. After that, Checker became the innovator of several new dances such as, *The Pony, Hucklebuck, Fly,* and *Limbo.* He has remained active in concert. His national hits include: *The Class, The Twist, The Hucklebuck, Whole Lotta Shakin' Goin' On, Pony Time, Dance the Mess Around, Let's Twist Again, The Fly, Slow Twistin', Dancin' Party, Limbo Rock, Popeye the Hitchhiker, Let's Limbo Some More, Twenty Miles, Birdland, Surf Party, Twist It Up, Loddy Lo, Hooka Tooka, Hey Bobba Needle, Lazy Elsie Molly, She Wants T'*

Swim, Lovely, Lovely, Do the Freddie, Hey You Little Boo-Ga-Loo, and *Back in the USSR.*

Linda Creed

She was a gifted lyricist who teamed with composer/producer Thom Bell in the era of Philly Soul. They collaborated on a number of hits for the Stylistics such as: *Stop, Look, Listen (To Your Heart), You Are Everything, Betcha by Golly Wow,* and *I'm Stone in Love With You.*

Creed and Bell also paired on a number of songs for the Spinners including the 1976 blockbuster: *The Rubberband Man.* In 1977 Creed teamed with composer Michael Masser to write *The Greatest Love of All* for the Muhammad Ali biopic: *The Greatest.* (The song topped the charts for Whitney Houston in 1986.) That same year Creed died from breast cancer while in her mid-thirties. In 1992, she was posthumously inducted into the Songwriters Hall of Fame.

Jim Croce

He was a gifted vocalist, guitarist, and composer. His most popular songs include: *Bad, Bad Leroy Brown* and *Time in a Bottle* (both reached No. 1). His other highly-charted hits are *You Don't Mess Around With Jim, I Got a Name, Operator,* and *I'll Have to Say I Love You in a Song.* His life and career were cut short by a fatal plane crash in 1973.

Danny and the Juniors

(Danny Rapp - Lead, Dave White, Frank Maffei, Joe Terranova (Terry).

The group got together at John Bartram High in Southwest Philadelphia and were called the Juvenairs. In 1957, group member Dave White wrote a song called *Let's All Do the Bop*, a popular dance at the time. Artie Singer of Singular Records, took the song to Dick Clark who suggested changing the lyrics and title. The song became *At the Hop* and the group became Danny and the Juniors. *At the Hop* became a No. 1 national hit. Their follow-up song *Rock And Roll Is Here to Stay* became an anthem for the music industry.

In the early 1960s, Dave White left the group and was replaced by Bill Carlucci. Their charted hits include *At the Hop, Sometimes (When I'm all Alone), Rock and Roll is Here to Stay, Dottie, Twistin' USA, Pony Express, Back to the Hop, Twistin' All Night Long, Doin' the Continental Walk,* and *Oo-La-La Limbo*.

A revised group led by Joe Terry is active today.

James Darren

Born and raised in South Philadelphia, he became a familiar face to audiences all over from his work in movies, television and the concert stage. After studying drama with Stella Adler in New York, he was discovered by Joyce Selznick. He signed a seven-year contract with Columbia Pictures and appeared in such films as *Rumble on the Docks, The Tijuana Story, The*

Brothers Rico, Gunmen's Walk, The Gene Krupa Story, and *Let No Man Write My Epitaph.* He also played the role of "Moondoggie" in the film *Gidget* and returned to star in two sequels. In *Gidget* he sang two songs, including the title tune, and became a major recording star.

His next hit, *Goodbye Cruel World* reached No. 1 on the charts and received a Grammy nomination. His other top ten releases included *Angel Face, Conscience,* and *Her Royal Majesty.*

In the early 1960s, Darren co-starred with Gregory Peck, Anthony Quinn, and David Niven in *The Guns of Navarone*, and with Charlton Heston in *Diamondhead.* In 1966 he starred in the sci-fi series, *The Time Tunnel* produced by Irwin Allen for ABC. In the 1970s, Darren toured with Buddy Hackett in concert throughout the country. He also guest-starred on TV in *Love - American Style, Policy Story, Hawaii Five-O, Charlie's Angels, S.W.A.T., The Black Sheep Squadron, Policewoman*, and *Fantasy Island.*

In 1982, Darren joined the cast of the ABC series *T.J. Hooker* as Officer Jim Corrigan. This provided the means for his next career move — directing. From the mid-1980s on, he directed such shows as *The A-Team, Hunter, Stingray, Police Story: Gladiator School (MOW), Diagnosis Murder, Walker, Texas Ranger, Raven, Renegade, Nowhere Man, Beverly Hills 90210, Melrose Place,* and *Savannah.* In 1998 he was cast as Vic Fontaine on *Star Trek: Deep Space Nine*, sang four standard tunes, and became a regular. This fostered his return to singing and recording.

Delfonics

Formed by brothers Wil and William Hart, the Grammy-winning group became known for their smooth singing, rich harmony, and skillful choreography, along with a unique sound of strings and French horns in the background. Some of their memorable songs include *La La Means I Love You, Didn't I Blow Your Mind, Hey Love, Break Your Promise, Somebody Loves You, I'm Sorry, Tell Me This is a Dream, He Really Don't Love You,* and *You Got Yours, I'll Get Mine.*

Bill Doggett

He formed his own band in 1938. In the late 1940s he worked as a musical arranger for Lionel Hampton, Louis Jordan, Count Basie, and Louis Armstrong. He also played piano for the Ink Spots.

In the early 1950s he formed his own combo and became known as one of the "fathers of the swinging organ." In 1956 he recorded his greatest seller, the instrumental *Honky-Tonk*. His other hits were *Ram-Bunk-Shush, Soft, Blip-Blop, Hold It,* and *Smokie.*

The Dovells

Len Borisoff (Barry), Jerry Gross (Summers), Arnie Silver (Satin), Mike Freda (Dennis), Mark Gordesky (Stevens), Jim Mealy (Danny Brooks)

They began singing in 1957 at local school functions. In 1961 Billy Harper brought a dance to the attention of Dave Appell and Kal Mann, where kids were stomping their feet to the beat of two popular songs: *Pretty Little Angel Eyes,* and *Every Day of the Week.* Appell and Mann wrote *The Bristol Stomp* which became the group's biggest hit. The Dovells' other charted hits include: *Do the New Continental, Bristol Twistin' Annie, Hully Gully Baby, You Can't Sit Down, Betty in Bermudas, The Jitterbug,* and *Stop Monkeyin' Around.*

In 1963 Len Barry left the group to become a solo artist. (He later had the hit *1-2-3.*) After his departure the group had charted songs with: *What in the World Has Come Over You, Dancin' in the Streets,* and *Here Come Da Judge* (as the Magistrates).

Today Jerry Gross and Mark Stevens continue to perform as the Dovells, blending music and comedy that creates a unique act and sets them apart from many of the standard groups from the 1960s rock 'n' roll era.

The Dreamlovers

(James Dunn, Clifford Dunn, Donald Hogan, Morris Gardner, Tommy Ricks and Cleveland Hammock, Jr.)

After backing up Chubby Checker on *The Twist*, and *Let's Twist Again*, The Dreamlovers became the resident back-up group at Cameo-Parkway. After recording hits with Dee Dee Sharp and the Dovells, the group had a major hit of their own, *When We Get Married*.

Fabian Forte

Discovered in his teens in 1958, Fabian was still a student at South Philadelphia High. His first release that year was a local hit called *Lillie Lou*. In 1959 he had a major hit with *I'm a Man*, and followed that with another huge hit, *Turn Me Loose*. With a magnetic presence, he became a teenage idol, and had a successful recording career with ten charted hits in a two year period.

In the early 1960s, Fabian turned his attention toward acting. He co-starred in 30 feature films and guest-starred on many network television series. In recent years, he has produced his own concert series for pay-per-view, public TV and syndication, and continues to make personal appearances throughout the country.

His charted hits include: *I'm a Man, Turn Me Loose, Tiger, Come on and Get Me, Got the Feeling, Hound Dog Man, This Friendly World, String Along, About This Thing Called Love*, and *Kissin' and Twistin'*.

His film credits include: *North to Alaska, High Time, Mr. Hobbs Takes a Vacation, Dear Brigette, The Longest Day,* Agatha Christie's *Ten Little Indians, Hound Dog Man, Thunder Alley, The Second Time Around, Wild Racers, Little Laura and Big John,* and Jules Verne's *Five Weeks in a Balloon.*

His many television credits include: *Bus Stop, Wagon Train, The Virginian, The Eleventh Hour, The Rat Patrol, The FBI, Laverne and Shirley, Facts of Life, The Love Boat, Murphy Brown, Blossom, Crisis in Mid-Air (MOW), Katie: Portrait of a Centerfold (MOW),* and *Getting Married (MOW).*

Eddie Fisher

As a child he sang in amateur singing contests and as a teen in local South Philadelphia clubs. In 1949, Fisher was discovered by Eddie Cantor while singing at Grossinger's Resort Hotel in the Catskills. In 1950 he signed a recording contract with RCA Victor and had his first hit: *Thinking of You.* In the early 1950s, Fisher became one of the most popular recording artists in the country.

A series of hits include: *Count Your Blessings, Heart, Dungaree Doll, Cindy Oh Cindy, Turn Back the Hand of Time, Anytime, Tell Me Why, Forgive Me, I'm Yours, Wish You Were Here, Lady of Spain, Even Now, Downhearted, I'm Walking Behind You, With These Hands, Many Times,* and *Oh My Papa.*

Four Aces

(Al Alberts - Lead, Dave Mahoney, Sod Vaccaro, Lou Silvestri)

After a recording of *Sin* in 1951, the group was signed by Decca Records. *Tell Me Why* became their first hit, and the Four Aces became a very popular singing group nationwide. Their songs were featured as title tunes in four motion pictures. In 1955 their recording of the title tune from the feature film *Love is a Many-Splendored Thing* became a No. 1 song.

Al Alberts left the group in the mid-1950s to become a solo act.

Their many hits include: *A Garden in the Rain, Perfidia, I'm Yours, Should I, Heart and Soul, Stranger in Paradise, The Gang That Sang Heart of My Heart, Three Coins in the Fountain, Wedding Bells, It's a Woman's World, Mister Sandman, Melody of Love, Heart, Love is a Many-Splendored Thing, A Woman In love, If You Can Dream, To Love Again, I Only Know I Love You, Friendly Persuasion, Someone to Love, Written on the Wind, Rock and Roll Rhapsody, The World Outside,* and *No Other Arms, No Other Lips.*

Sunny Gale

Born and raised in a South Philadelphia neighborhood of future singers, she became a successful recording artist in the pre-rock 1950s. Although a number of her songs were covered by other artists, she became a solid hit-maker for RCA Victor. Her charted hits were: *Wheel of Fortune, I Laughed at Love,*

Teardrops on My Pillow, A Stolen Waltz, Love Me Again, Before It's Too Late, Goodnight Sweetheart Goodnight, Smile, and *Let Me Go Lover.* She continued recording until the early 1960s.

Kenny Gamble

A two-time Grammy Award winner and legendary contributor to many hit records and albums, Gamble began his career as part of "The Romeos," a singing group in the early 1960s. Later he became a prolific songwriter-producer with Camden native **Leon Huff**. Together, Gamble and Huff originated the legendary "Philly Soul Sound" of the 1970s. Some of their greatest releases include: *Expressway to Your Heart, Cowboys to Girls, Only the Strong Survive, Me and Mrs. Jones, If You Don't Know Me by Now, Love Train,* and *Ain't No Stoppin' Us Now.*

In recent years, Kenny Gamble and his wife have been very active in urban renewal, rebuilding and revitalizing the inner city neighborhoods of Philadelphia.

Charlie Gracie

He first learned to play guitar as a youth growing up in South Philadelphia. At age 14, he made an impressive debut on Paul Whiteman's TV Teen Club, and became a regular on the show for two years. In 1951, Gracie recorded what some consider the first rock 'n' roll record: *Boogie Woogie Blues.* In 1957, a 20-year-old Gracie recorded *Butterfly,* written by Bernie Lowe and Kal Mann. The song became a No. 1 hit and sold over 3 million copies in the U.S. and U.K. The flip side, *99 Ways*, charted at No. 11 to make the record a double-sided hit. Gracie's follow-up, *Fabulous*, reached No. 16 on the charts to give him 3 top-rated releases in the same year.

His other songs did well in England also, where his recordings of *I Love You So Much It Hurts*, and *Wanderin' Eyes* charted at 14 and 6 respectively. He achieved a total of 7 top 20 hits there.

Known as a virtuoso guitar player, Gracie was highly admired by George Harrison and Paul McCartney who recorded *Fabulous* on one of his recent albums. Gracie still performs to large audiences throughout Europe and England.

Buddy Greco

He's enjoyed a lengthy career as a singer, songwriter, arranger and producer. Born in South Philadelphia, he studied piano at the Philadelphia Settlement House. At age 15 he had his own musical group. In 1946 his trio (Buddy Greco with the Sharps) had their first big hit, *Oh Look at Her, Ain't She Pretty.* In 1948, Greco joined the Benny Goodman Band as a piano player-vocalist-arranger.

In the early 1950s he appeared on TV and wrote songs for artists Rosemary Clooney and Eileen Barton. Between 1951 and 1955 he recorded a dozen songs for Coral Records including the best seller, *I Ran All the Way Home.* In the 1960s he recorded a number of popular albums and in 1967 had his own TV series on CBS with Buddy Rich called *Away We Go*.

In the 1970s, Greco moved to Europe and performed around the world. After returning to the U.S., he continued to perform, produce, write and arrange.

Bill Haley and His Comets

Bill Haley, Billy Williamson (steel guitar), Franny Beecher (lead guitar), Johnny Grande (accordion-piano), Marshall Lytle (Bass), Joey Ambrose (sax), Dick Richards (drums).

The group had their first hit in 1953 with *Crazy Man Crazy*. The following year they had two million sellers in *Shake Rattle and Roll* and *Dim Dim the Lights*. In 1955, a song they had recorded over a year earlier, *(We're Gonna) Rock Around the Clock,* found new life as the theme song for the movie *Blackboard Jungle*. It became the No. 1 song in the world. Often called the *Father of Rock 'n' Roll*, Haley opened the door for many groups to follow.

Charted hits include: *Crazy Man Crazy, Shake Rattle and Roll, Dim Dim the Lights, Mambo Rock, Birth of the Boogie, (We're Gonna) Rock Around the Clock, Razzle Dazzle, Two Hound Dogs, Burn That Candle, See You Later Alligator, Rock, The Saints Rock 'n' Roll, Hot Dog Buddy Buddy, Rip It Up, Rudy's Rock, Forty Cups of Coffee, Billy Goat, Skinny Minnie, Lean Jean, Joey's Song.*

Hall and Oates

Daryl Hall was a back-up singer with several soul groups before meeting John Oates at Temple University where both were students in 1967. They began singing together in 1972. Their first charted single was *She's Gone* in 1974, followed by *Sara Smile* in 1976. The following year, their recording of *Rich Girl* rose to No. 1, and six more charted hits followed.

In the 1980s they became the top rock duo of the decade, with five No. 1 songs: *Kiss on My List, I Can't Go for That, Private Eyes, Maneater,* and *Out of Touch.* Their top ten hits include: *You Make My Dreams, Do It in a Minute, One on One, Family Man, Say It Isn't So, Adult Education, Method of Modern Love,* and *Everything Your Heart Desires.*

Douglas "Jocko" Henderson
(Your Ace from Outer Space)

He was said to have had one of the most unique and pleasant voices in the broadcasting industry. He began his career at WBAL in Baltimore, then came to WHAT in Philadelphia. He later moved to WDAS and at one time was on the air in both Philly and New York (WDV). In 1970, Henderson started a local magazine called "Philly Talk." He also produced and promoted records. In later years, he spent time promoting his *Get Ready* program for school districts around the country, where he recorded himself teaching everything from math to American history with rap lyrics.

Eddie Holman

While attending Overbrook High School in the early 1960s, he began to write, produce and record. His first charted hit was *This Can't Be True Girl.* Other popular recordings include *Eternal Love, Time Will Tell, It's All in the Game, I Love You, United,* and *Don't Stop Now.* His recording of *Hey There Lonely Girl* is one of the top selling and best remembered romantic ballads of all time. Holman's falsetto style of singing has earned him a unique place in soul music history. Today he travels internationally with the Eddie Holman Band.

Ed Hurst

Born and raised in Atlantic City, he originated the 950 Club with partner Joe Grady on WPEN in post-war Philadelphia. It was the first teenage dance show on the air. In the early 1950s, Hurst moved his show to TV and was broadcast every Saturday. In the mid-1950s, Grady and Hurst had a daily TV show from Wilmington that rivaled Bandstand. In 1960, their *Summertime on the Pier* began airing on WRCV-TV and became a fixture every summer weekend for nearly two decades.

In the 1980s Hurst returned to WPEN with Partner Joe Grady to host the 950 Club. When Grady retired in 1987, Ed Hurst remained on the air almost 50 years after it all began.

The Intruders

They were four Philadelphians: **Sam "Little Sonny" Brown, Eugene "Bird" Daughtry, Phillip "Phil" Terry, and Robert "Big Sonny" Edwards,** who began singing together in the early 1960s. The group blended Philly's street-corner doo-wop tradition with Black gospel influence that attracted Kenny Gamble and Leon Huff, who signed them to Philadelphia International Records. In 1970 Robert "Bobby Star" Ferguson joined the group. Some of their best sellers were *Cowboys to Girls, (Love is Like a) Baseball Game, When We Get Married, (Win, Place or Show) She's a Winner,* and *I'll Always Love My Mama.*

Jodimars
Joey Ambrose, Dick Richards, Marshall Lytle

They left Bill Haley & His Comets in late 1955 to form their own group (Jodimars) which was taken from their first names.

They signed with Capitol Records in 1956 and their first release *Now Dig This* was a national hit. This was followed by *Let's All Rock Together,* and *Clarabella* (which was later recorded by the Beatles and used in their concert series).

In the late '50s, Jodimars became one of the top lounge acts in Las Vegas and Reno. They also enjoyed widespread popularity in Europe and the U.K. where *Now Dig This* became the title of the well-known English rock magazine.

Kitty Kallen

As a youth she performed on the Children's Hour on WCAU radio, and was discovered by band leader Gil Fitch, who also played for the SPHAS (Philadelphia's first pro basketball team). In the late 1930s, Kallen was a teenage songstress with Fitch and his band at the Broadwood Hotel after Saturday night SPHA games.

In the 1940s she became a band singer with Jimmy Dorsey and Harry James. In the early 1950s Kallen signed with Decca Records, and in 1954 had a No. 1 hit with *Little Things Mean a Lot*. After a brief retirement, in the late '50s, she signed with Columbia Records. She had a hit soon after with *If I Give My Heart to You*. Other charted songs include *In the Chapel in the Moonlight, I Want You All to Myself, Go on With the Wedding* (with Georgie Shaw), and *My Coloring Book* in 1963.

Patti LaBelle

Born and raised in the melting pot of Southwest Philadelphia, she has enjoyed a long-lasting musical career. She grew up singing in a local Baptist choir. In the early 1960s she became the lead singer of the Bluebelles, and the group had four charted hits by 1965. In the 1970s, LaBelle launched a solo career and has amassed over 30 charted singles. They include 1975's *Lady Marmalade*, 1983's chart topper, *If You Only Knew,* the 1985 hit *New Attitude*, a pop and R&B No. 1 single *On My Own* (which was a 1986 duet with Michael McDonald), and more recent hits like *Somebody Loves You Baby, When You've Been Blessed, The Right Kind of Lover,* and *When You Talk About Love.*

Her solo works include the platinum-selling *Winner in You,* and three gold albums, *Burnin', Gems,* and *Flame.* LaBelle has also authored four books including her best-selling autobiography, *Don't Block the Blessings.* A multiple Grammy Award winner, she last received a nomination in 2003 for the inspirational hit *Way Up There.* In 2004 she recorded the album *Timeless Journey* and began hosting the new TV series: *Living It Up.*

Mario Lanza

Born and raised in South Philadelphia, he began singing as a teenager while in his high school choir. After serving in the military, he returned home and signed a ten year recording contract with RCA Victor. In 1949 he made his film debut for MGM in *That Midnight Kiss.* The following year, in the film *Toast of New Orleans,* Lanza sang *Be My Love.* It became a No. 1 national hit in 1951. A year later, his portrayal of Enrico Caruso in *The Great Caruso* brought him worldwide recognition.

In the late 1950s he went to Europe to make a series of films. In 1959 he died of a heart attack at age 38. His greatest hits were: *Be My Love, Vesti la Giubba, The Loveliest Night of the Year, Because You're Mine, Earthbound,* and *Arrivederci Roma.*

Hy Lit (Hyski Orooni McVouty Ozoot)

He's been termed the voice of Philadelphia radio over the past 45 years, taking his listeners uptown, downtown, and crosstown. A pioneer of rock 'n' roll radio, Lit became a Philadelphia phenomenon on WIBG (99 AM) during his nightly 6 to 10 PM shift. He later had his own television show.

His popularity kept him in demand at dance halls and clubs across the Delaware Valley. In the 1970s he served as Master of Ceremonies for the Harlem Globetrotters all across the country. In recent years, Lit has been in residence at WOGL (98.1 FM) playing the "oldies."

Little Joe and the Thrillers
Joe Cook (lead), Harry Pascle, Farris Hill, Donald Burnett, Richard Frazier

In 1957, Joe Cook and his group recorded a song he had written called *Peanuts*. The song became a national hit on Okeh Records.

The Majors
Ricky Cordo (lead), Frank Trout, Ronald Gathers, Eugene Glass, Idella Morris

With a distinct sound, the group had major success with *A Wonderful Dream* in 1962 on Imperial Records.

Gloria Mann

She was one of the better-known female vocalists to emerge from Philadelphia in the mid-1950s. In 1956 her recording of *Teenage Prayer* placed in the top 20. Other memorable songs were *Earth Angel* and *Goodnight, Sweetheart, Goodnight.* Some of her best work was covered by other artists preventing her from reaching the mega-stardom she might have achieved.

Peggy March

She began singing as a child and was a regular on the Rex Trailer TV Show in the mid-1950s. After that, she sang in local bands. In 1963, while still a high school student, she recorded *I Will Follow Him* for RCA, that rose to No. 1. Her other charted hits include: *I Wish I Were a Princess, Hello Heartache Goodbye Love, The Impossible Happened,* and *Every Little Move You Make.*

The success of *I Will Follow Him* gave her opportunities abroad, and she began to record in Dutch, Italian, Spanish, Japanese and German. Through the 1960s she continually topped the German charts and enjoyed success in Japan as well.

In the 1970s, she lived in Germany and began writing songs. In 1981 she co-authored two hits: *Manuel Goodbye* and *When the Rain Begins to Fall.* March eventually returned to the U.S. and continues to appear in concert. In recent years she has become an accomplished painter.

Al Martino

He became one of South Philadelphia's finest pop singers and began his recording career with Capitol Records in 1952. His first hit, *Here in My Heart*, went to No. 1. His other charted hits in the 1950s and 1960s include *Take My Heart, Rachel, I Can't Get You Out of My Heart, Darling I Love You, I Love You Because, Painted Tainted Rose, Living a Lie, I Love you More and More Each Day, Always Together, Tears and Roses* and *We Could.* In 1966 he recorded *Spanish Eyes* which became his signature song.

His portrayal of Johnny Fontaine in *The Godfather* and his recording of *Speak Softly Love* (the film's love theme) refreshed his career in the 1970s. He continued to perform in clubs, lounges and casinos for many years after. In 2000, he recorded the album *Style*. His latest CD is *Come Share the Wine*.

Joe Niagara (The Rockin' Bird)

As a South Philadelphia youth, he grew up wanting to be a radio announcer. After being discharged from the service at age 19, he began working at WDAS in 1947. After filing records at the station, Niagara was given the chance to introduce some records on the air, and his wish came true. Two years later, he landed a job at WIBG and remained there for ten years.

In the late 1950s, Niagara was one of the top rock 'n' roll D.J.s in Philadelphia. After a three year stint at KBIG in Los Angeles, he returned to WIBG and remained there for the 1960s.

In the mid-1970s he came to WPEN and remained on the air for 25 years.

The Orlons
Shirley Brickley, Rosetta Hightower, Marlena Davis and Stephen Caldwell

The group got together while in their teens at Overbrook High and began to appear in talent shows at school with a group called the Cashmeres (who became the Dovells). While looking for a group name, Stephen Caldwell had a black orlon sweater that he showed to the group. After seeing it, they decided to call themselves the Orlons (a similar name in material to cashmere).

Len Barry, lead singer of the Dovells, arranged an audition for the group with Cameo. At the first audition, Caldwell sang lead with the three girls backgrounding. Cameo-Parkway requested a second audition where Shirley Brickley, Rosetta Hightower and Marlena Davis each led a song. The group was then signed to a contract.

Their first release, *I'll Be True*, was a local hit with Davis singing lead. Their second local hit, *Mr. Twenty One*, had Brickley in the lead. Their biggest seller came in 1962 with *Wah Watusi*, written by Dave Appell and Kal Mann with Rosetta Hightower singing lead.

Other charted songs include *Don't Hang Up, South Street, Not Me, Crossfire, Bon-Doo-Wah, Shimmy Shimmy, Rules of Love,* and *Knock-Knock.*

Today, Stephen Caldwell leads a revised group that includes Jean Brickley, Alberta Crump and Madeline Morris.

Mike Pedicin

A talented guitarist, Pedicin made numerous appearances on Bandstand and had two charted hits in the mid-1950s: *Large, Large House* (RCA) and *Shake a Hand* (Cameo).

Teddy Pendergrass

In the early 1970s he became the lead singer of Harold Melvin and the Blue Notes. He left the group in 1976 to go solo, and with a surging baritone, became one of the top R&B artists in the country. His first three albums went gold or platinum. A 1982 car accident left him partially paralyzed, but after a year of rehabilitation he returned to the music scene. He continued to record albums through the 1980s and 1990s, some of which went gold. His memorable songs include: *I Don't Love You Anymore, You Can't Hide from Yourself, The More I Get the More I Want,* and the huge hit, *Close the Door.*

Todd Rundgren

He became a virtuoso musician, songwriter, and producer. Formerly the lead of the groups Nazz and Utopia. His mega-hits include: *Hello It's Me, I Saw the Light,* and *We Gotta Get You a Woman.* Other charted songs include *Couldn't I Just Tell You, A*

Dream Goes on Forever, Real Man, Be Nice to Me, Good Vibrations, and *Can We Still Be Friends.*

Bobby Rydell

He learned to play drums as a child after seeing Gene Krupa at the Earle Theater. By age 10, he was a regular on Paul Whiteman's TV Teen Club on WFIL. As a teen, he played drums, sang and did impersonations in a group called Rocco and the Saints. He signed with Cameo Records in 1959 at age 17, scored big with the record *Kissin' Time* and had over 20 charted hits including million sellers such as *Wild One, Volare* and *Forget Him.*

In 1963 Rydell co-starred with Ann-Margret in the film version of *Bye Bye Birdie.* He later recorded with Capitol Records and in the 1970s moved more into the "pop area." In the 1980s Rydell joined Frankie Avalon and Fabian on a national tour. In the 1990s he appeared in big-band style concert dates and on a number of TV specials.

His charted hits include *Kissin' Time, We Got Love, I Dig Girls, Wild One, Little Bitty Girl, Swingin' School, Ding-a-Ling, Volare, Sway, Goodtime Baby, I've Got Bonnie, I'll Never Dance Again, That Old Black Magic, I Wanna Thank You, The Fish, The Cha-Cha-Cha, Butterfly Baby, Wildwood Days, Forget Him, Make Me Forget, A World Without Love, I Just Can't Say Goodbye,* and *Diana.*

Jodie Sands

She was discovered by Bob Marcucci and Peter DeAngelis in 1957. Her recording of *With All My Heart* became one of Chancellor Records' first hits. Her follow-up, *Someday*, was also a national hit.

The Sensations
Yvonne Baker (lead), Richard Curtain, Sam Armstrong, Alphonso Howell

In the mid 1950s the group was formed by Baker and Howell. They had a hit with *Yes Sir, That's My Baby* for Atco Records. Baker retired but rejoined the group in 1961. That summer they recorded *Music, Music, Music* for Argo Records that made the national charts. Their biggest success came the following year with a song written by Yvonne Baker called *Let Me In*. They recorded their final hit that year with *That's My Desire*.

Dee Dee Sharp

She grew up in North Philadelphia and learned to play piano by age 10. She then began directing the choir at the church of her grandfather, Pastor Eubie Gilbert. At age 12, when her mother was severely injured in an automobile accident, she looked for work to help her family. She answered a newspaper ad and became a background singer to Willa Ward (sister of Clara Ward, the first gospel singer to appear in nightclubs). With the skills she developed, Sharp worked on sessions with Frankie Avalon, Fabian,

Bobby Rydell, and Chubby Checker. Her big break came in 1962 when her vocals were added to Chubby Checker's *Slow Twistin'* making it a duet. At 16 she recorded *Mashed Potato Time* and became an overnight sensation.

Her many appearances on American Bandstand and at teen dances made her the first black female teenage idol in the early 1960s. In later years she did concert and club dates and became a very popular nightclub performer. Her other charted singles include: *Gravy, Ride, Do the Bird, Wild,* and *I Really Love You.* Her later hits include *I'm Not in Love* (from the *Happy 'Bout the Whole Thing* album from which she wrote the title cut), *I'd Really Love to See You Tonight* (from the CD *What Color is Love*), and *Breaking and Entering* and *I Love You Anyway* (from the CD *Dee Dee* produced by Jerry Butler).

She also appeared in Donald Byrd's *Nutcracker*, and in Billy Dee Williams' *Brown Sugar.* In recent years she has written commercials and been the spokesperson for "Shades of You" by Maybelline.

Georgie Shaw

He garnered acclaim for a number of hits in the mid-1950s. Among them: *Rags to Riches, No Arms Can Ever Hold You, Go on With the Wedding* (with Kitty Kallen), *Faded Summer Love,* and *To You My Love.*

The Sherrys

Joe Cook, who was the lead singer of *Little Joe and the Thrillers*, formed a singing group that consisted of his two daughters and two of their friends. The girls recorded two hits in the early 1960s: *Pop, Pop Pop-Pie* and *Slop Time.*

The Silhouettes

Earl Beal, Raymond Edwards, Bill Horton and Rick Lewis were an R&B harmony vocal group that scored big in 1957 with *Get a Job*, considered by many to be the "doo-wop" song of the 1950s (written by group member Rick Lewis). They continued to perform through the 1960s with two of the four original members.

Artie Singer

As a musician, bandleader, songwriter and voice teacher, he was instrumental in developing the talents of Al Martino, James Darren, Chubby Checker, Bobby Rydell, and Dee Dee Sharp. In recent times, he has composed and presented a Broadway musical with lyrics by Marjorie Baderak and libretto by Lisa and Sherry Gresson, and collaborated with Roy Straigis on a new PAX TV children's series: *Gina D's Kids Club.*

The Stylistics

Began as a group in the late 1960s. The original members were **Russell Thompkins, Jr., Airrion Love, James Smith,**

James Dunn, and Herb Murrell. With a unique sound and identity, The Stylistics had a string of 12 top 10 releases through the 1970s. Their memorable songs include: *You Make Me Feel Brand New, I'm Stone in Love With You, Break Up to Make Up, People Make the World Go Round, Betcha by Golly Wow, Stop Look Listen (To Your Heart), You Are Everything, You'll Never Get to Heaven (If You Break My Heart), Rockin' Roll Baby, Can't Give You Anything (But My Love),* and *You're a Big Girl Now.*

Tammi Terrell

As a beautiful teen with gifted vocal ability, she won a number of local talent contests and became the opening club act for performers such as Gary U.S. Bonds and Patti LaBelle and the Bluebelles. In the early 1960s she made her recording debut with *If You See Bill,* followed by *The Voice of Experience.* She later recorded *I Cried* for James Brown's Try Me label and toured with his revue. In 1965 at age 20, while performing with Jerry Butler in Detroit, she caught the attention of Berry Gordy, Jr. and signed with Motown Records.

After recording the R&B singles: *Come on and See Me, This Old Heart of Mine,* and *Hold Me Oh My Darling*, she was paired with Marvin Gaye. Together they created some of the greatest love songs ever to emerge from Motown. Their classic duets were *Ain't No Mountain High Enough, Ain't Nothin' Like the Real Thing*, and *You're All I Need to Get By.* Tragically, she died at age 24, as the result of a brain tumor.

Three Degrees
Sheila Ferguson, Valerie Holiday, Helen Scott

The group was discovered by producer-songwriter Richard Barrett in 1963. Two original members, Fayette Pickney and Linda Turner, left the group that same year and were replaced by Helen Scott and Janet Jones who sang with Shirley Porter. In the mid-1960s Scott and Jones left and were replaced by Sheila Ferguson and Valerie Holiday.

In 1970, the group had their first national hit with a remake of *Maybe* (a classic hit by the Chantels), with Helen Scott returning to do the lead vocals. The song reached No. 4, and their follow-up: *I Do Take You* reached No. 7.

After signing with Gamble and Huff's Philadelphia International Records in 1973, the group had a disco hit called *Dirty O' Man*. In 1974 they did the vocal track for *TSOP* (The Sound of Philadelphia) which was recorded by MFSB as the theme song for the TV show *Soul Train*. Released as a single, it went gold and hit No. 1. That same year they recorded *When Will I See You Again* which went platinum and sold over 2 million copies. Their follow-up *I Didn't Know* was a big hit in 1975.

The Trammps
Jimmy Ellis-lead, Harold Wade, Stanley Wade, Earl Young

In the 1970s they emerged in the spotlight. Their first charted hit was *Zing Went the Strings of My Heart* (a remake of

Judy Garland's 1940s tune). Other hits followed: *Hold Back the Night, Where Do We Go from Here,* and *Where the Happy People Go.* In 1977, they scored with *Disco Inferno* (featured in the film *Saturday Night Fever),* which won them a Grammy Award.

The Turbans
Al Banks (lead), Matthew Platt, Charles Williams, Andrew Jones

They began performing in the mid-1950s, and recorded a song bass singer Andrew Jones had written called *When You Dance* which became their biggest hit. Other charted singles include: *Sister Sookey, B-I-N-G-O, It Was a Night Like This, Valley of Love,* and *The Wadda-do.*

The Tymes
Donald Banks, Al (Caesar) Berry, Norman Burnett, George Hilliard, George Williams, Jr.

They began singing in 1957 at record hops and local clubs. In 1963 they appeared on a WDAS Talent Show: Tip Top Talent Hunt, and were heard by an executive at Parkway. A month later, they recorded a song written by George Williams, Roy Straigis and Billy Jackson called *So Much in Love,* which became a No. 1 national hit. Other memorable songs include *Wonderful! Wonderful!, Somewhere, To Each His Own, Here She Comes* and

People. Today, the original group with new members Lafayette Gamble and Jimmy Wells, do concert dates all over the U.S.

Joe Valino

Born and raised in South Philadelphia, he reached the charts in 1956 with *Garden of Eden.*

Virtues
Frank Virtue (lead guitar), Jimmy Bruno (guitar), Ralph Frederico (piano) Barry Smith (drums)

Virtue formed the group in the late 1940s. They played on radio and by the mid-1950s on TV. They recorded a song called *Guitar Boogie Shuffle* that became a hit in 1959.

Georgie Woods (the Guy with the Goods)

He became a legendary broadcasting personality in the City of Philadelphia. In a career that covered decades on WHAT and WDAS radio, he also staged legendary rock shows at the Uptown Theater in North Philadelphia, and contributed much of his time to community needs. Along the way, Woods improved, enhanced and inspired the lives of many in his multi-faceted career of entertainment and public service.

About the Author

Born and raised in Northwest Philadelphia, James Rosin graduated from Temple University's School of Communications with a degree in broadcasting. In New York, he studied acting with Bobby Lewis, appeared in plays off-off Broadway, and on the ABC soap opera *Edge of Night*. In Los Angeles, he played featured and co-starring roles in episodic TV shows such as *Mike Hammer, T.J. Hooker, Quincy M.E., General Hospital, The Powers of Matthew Star, Cannon, Mannix, Banacek, Adam-12, Love - American Style*, and two mini-series: *Loose Change* and *Once An Eagle*. He also wrote stories and teleplays for *Quincy M.E.* (NBC), *Capitol* (CBS) and *Loving Friends and Perfect Couples* (Showtime). His full-length play *Michael in Beverly Hills* premiered at Don Eitner's American Theater Arts in Los Angeles, and was later presented off-off Broadway.

In recent years he wrote and produced two one-hour sports documentaries that have aired on public television: *Philly Hoops: The SPHAS and Warriors* (about the first two professional basketball teams in Philadelphia) and *The Philadelphia Athletics 1901-1954* (about the former American League franchise). His first book, *Philly Hoops: The SPHAS and Warriors,* was published in October of 2003.